A BEGINNER'S GUIDE TO
RECOGNIZING TREES
OF THE
NORTHEAST

"I've lived with trees, studied trees, and designed with trees my whole life. This is the best work for tree identification I have ever seen. Mikolas's unique approach takes the complexity out of the undertaking and imparts a familiarity with each tree that is normally only hard-won through experience."

—Laurie E. Klenkel, PLA, Landscape Architect

A BEGINNER'S GUIDE TO RECOGNIZING TREES OF THE NORTHEAST

INCLUDING CONNECTICUT, INDIANA, MAINE, MASSACHUSETTS, MICHIGAN, NEW HAMPSHIRE, NEW JERSEY, NEW YORK, OHIO, PENNSYLVANIA, RHODE ISLAND, VERMONT, AND WEST VIRGINIA

MARK MIKOLAS

The Countryman Press
A division of W. W. Norton & Company
Independent Publishers Since 1923

For information about permission to reproduce selections
from this book, write to Permissions, The Countryman Press,
500 Fifth Avenue, New York, NY 10110

For information about special discounts for bulk purchases,
please contact W. W. Norton Special Sales at
specialsales@wwnorton.com or 800-233-4830

All maps from E. L. Little, Jr., *Atlas of United States Trees, Vol. 1: Conifers
and Important Hardwoods*. U.S. Department of Agriculture Miscellaneous
Publication 1146 (1971). Via gec.cr.usgs.gov/data/little/

Manufacturing by Versa Press
Book design by Endpaper Studio
Production manager: Devon Zahn

Library of Congress Cataloging-in-Publication Data

Names: Mikolas, Mark, 1945– author.
Title: A beginner's guide to recognizing trees of
the Northeast / Mark Mikolas.
Description: New York, NY : The Countryman Press, [2017]
Identifiers: LCCN 2017025434 | ISBN 9781682681107 (pbk.)
Subjects: LCSH: Trees—Northeastern States—Identification.
Classification: LCC QK117 .M55 2017 | DDC 582.16—dc23
LC record available at https://lccn.loc.gov/2017025434

The Countryman Press
www.countrymanpress.com

A division of W. W. Norton & Company
500 Fifth Avenue, New York, NY 10110
www.wwnorton.com

10 9 8 7 6 5 4 3

CONTENTS

ACKNOWLEDGMENTS 7

INTRODUCTION 9

DECIDUOUS TREES

1. Red maple 15
2. Sugar maple 21
3. *How to tell red maple from sugar maple* 27
4. Beech 31
5. Ash 39
6. *How to tell maple from ash* 43
7. Aspen 45
8. Cottonwood 51
9. Yellow birch 55
10. Red oak 59
11. *How to tell red oak from beech in the winter* 67
12. White oak 69
13. *How to tell red oak from white oak* 73
14. Shagbark hickory 75
15. Yellow poplar 79
16. Tupelo 81
17. Basswood 87
18. Apple 91
19. Willow 95
20. Paper birch 97
21. Gray birch 103
22. *How to tell paper birch from gray birch* 107
23. Black birch 109
24. River birch 113
25. Black cherry 115

26. *How to tell black cherry from black birch* **117**

27. Pin cherry **119**

28. Striped maple **121**

29. Sycamore **125**

30. Black locust **131**

31. Hornbeam **137**

32. Hophornbeam **139**

33. Ironwood **141**

34. Black walnut **143**

35. Slippery elm **149**

36. American elm **153**

37. Staghorn sumac **155**

CONIFEROUS TREES

38. Pines **161**

39. White pine **163**

40. Red pine **169**

41. Pitch pine **175**

42. Hemlock **179**

43. Balsam fir **185**

44. Spruce **189**

45. *How to tell spruce from balsam fir* **193**

46. Cedar **195**

47. Tamarack **199**

STATE TREES **203**

CHAMPION TREES **205**

ACKNOWLEDGMENTS

Much of what I have learned over the years has come from my good friends Jeff Nugent and Bill Guenther. With them I have hiked many miles throughout the Northeast, always observing and talking about the trees we encountered. My thanks also go out to my many other hiking friends for their patience both with my persistent questioning and my many stops to photograph.

INTRODUCTION

WHY DOES THE WORLD NEED ANOTHER TREE GUIDE?

A large number of guides for tree identification already exist. Almost all depend on leaves and other features, such as fruit, nuts, buds, flowers, bud scars, and silhouettes. Many guides include hundreds of trees, and they often cover very large geographies, such as the Eastern United States or the whole country. In addition, many take pride in emphasizing fine distinctions between closely related species.

What is wrong with these guides? Nothing. Except that they can be very confusing and hard to use for someone unfamiliar with tree identities to begin with. As Philip Werner writes in the blog *SectionHiker*: "I learned yesterday that tree identification for novices is not as easy as I had hoped. I managed to identify a few tree species . . . but then things got real confusing. There were a lot of species I simply couldn't identify in the tree book I had brought along with me."

There are other problems. Northern deciduous trees have no leaves in the winter; fruit, nuts, and flowers appear only at a certain time of year; if a tree's branches are far above your head, you cannot see small details like buds or bud scars; silhouettes vary enormously depending on the specific conditions in which a tree grows; and even trying to identify a tree by its leaves can be confusing when faced with the variety of options in a thorough guide. For instance, the *Checklist of United States Trees*, published by the U.S. Forest Service, lists more than 150 oaks. A popular tree guide to Eastern trees lists over 40 oaks, still an overwhelming number for beginners and even seasoned amateur naturalists.

Why does the world need another tree guide? As small children, we all learned the names of many things, such as animals, fruits, and dinosaurs, but no cultural experience familiarized us with the names of trees. Many adults love trees, but may feel a little guilty about not recognizing them by name. Those who would like to be able to recognize more trees need an easy resource to begin learning about them. This guide intends to fill that need.

HOW CAN TREE IDENTIFICATION BE MADE EASIER?

We make identification easy by restricting the geography covered, by reducing the number of trees we focus on, by selecting the key features needed to identify a tree, and by avoiding fine distinctions.

HOW WE RESTRICT THE GEOGRAPHY

We reduce the number of trees we focus on by restricting the geography to one area where similar types of trees can be found. This book covers the Northeast, but as it turns out, there are many different combinations of states that are called "the Northeast": the Census Bureau has one, the Association of American Geographers has another, U.S. Fish and Wildlife has yet another, the Library of Congress has its own, and so on. The definition we are using, shown below, follows that of the World Geographical Scheme for Recording Plant Distributions, which maps a common zone in which similar plants and trees can thrive. This zone stretches from Maine south to West Virginia and west to Indiana and Michigan, as shown on the map.

The Northeast, as defined by the World Geographical Scheme for Recording Plant Distributions.

HOW WE REDUCE THE NUMBER OF TREES WE FOCUS ON

You do not have to learn every tree in the forest to recognize most of them. In fact, the first dozen species of deciduous trees in this book (those that lose leaves in the winter) together make up about 95 percent of all the deciduous trees in the Northeast. The eight conifers covered here represent nearly 100 percent of all conifers to be encountered in the Northeast. That means that if you learn 12 deciduous trees and eight conifers, you will recognize the vast majority of the trees that you will encounter.

We also do not make fine distinctions between species. For instance, among others, there are white, black, green, and blue ashes, but by far the most prevalent is white ash, so that is what is included here. Likewise, not all trees commonly known as cedar are even in the same genus, but if you can identify one type of cedar, you will recognize the others as well. Thus we do not distinguish among them.

HOW WE SELECT THE KEY FEATURES NEEDED FOR IDENTIFICATION

Foresters can walk through a wood and identify which tree is which with little more than a glance. How do they do that—even in the winter, when there are no leaves? They almost unconsciously focus on a few keys to identification. These keys may include location, bark, color, form of growth, and so on. We use the same ability when we pick someone we know well out of a crowd of people, even if we cannot see their face.

For each tree, I have identified and then focused on those key factors that lead to easy identification. For instance, once you have learned that black cherry is the only tree whose bark looks as if burnt potato chips have been pasted all over it—and you have seen some photos illustrating that fact—you will ever after be able to identify black cherry trees and know that you are right. This approach is simple and straightforward, and it works year round.

HOW WE AVOID FINE DISTINCTIONS

When someone is learning something, it is necessary to simplify in the beginning. For instance, we might tell young students that the Boston Tea Party led to the American Revolution. That is not wrong, but historians see a much more complicated series of events and have written detailed and scholarly treatises on the subject. Similarly for trees, we simplify at the beginning. There are many statements made in this book that are true, but a botanist or a dendrologist (a scientist who studies wooded plants) would say, "but, but, but . . ." because they know that far more detailed information is needed to completely clarify an identification or because they want to correct the language to conform to scientific rigor. If you want the botanist's point of view, then other guides are far more suitable. In this book, we aim for simplicity so beginners can learn how to recognize trees.

HOW TO USE THIS GUIDE

This guide classifies trees as either deciduous (losing leaves in the winter) or coniferous (having cones and needles). The first twelve species are the most frequently encountered trees, listed in the order of their overall numbers, red maple being the most common. Similar families of trees appear in sequence, and special sections are added to clear up common points of confusion.

You take most guides with you into the field, and when you see a tree you want to identify, you try to look it up in the guide. This book is meant to work in reverse: First, study the book and learn the keys to a tree or two, and then go into the field looking for them. When you find one, look closely at it, become familiar with its features, and then locate more. Soon you will be able to recognize that tree whenever you encounter it.

Do not worry about failing to recognize a tree. Trees do not always make it easy for us: There is a great deal of variation in the color and pattern of their bark, and their appearance can change dramatically as they grow from saplings into mature trees. Clearly, you should not expect these identification keys to work with every tree. When you are unsure, just move on. The object is to find trees you *can* recognize.

As Thomas Hardy wrote in *Under the Greenwood Tree*, "To dwellers in a wood, almost every species of tree has its voice as well as its feature." Soon, you will begin recognizing their voices and features and start feeling more at one with the community of trees around us.

DECIDUOUS TREES

We had not gone far before I was startled by seeing what I thought was an Indian encampment, covered with a red flag, on the bank, and exclaimed, "Camp!" to my comrades. I was slow to discover that it was a red maple changed by the frost.

—Henry David Thoreau, *The Maine Woods*

1 RED MAPLE

Soft maple, swamp maple

Red maple is called *red* because its twigs, buds, and flowers are all red, and its leaves turn a flaming red in the fall—in fact, its leaves are among the earliest in the fall to start turning. It is also the most widespread deciduous tree in the eastern U.S., able to grow in wet and dry conditions, poor and rich soils, and in bottomlands and at elevation.

WHERE TO LOOK FOR RED MAPLE

According to the USDA Forest Service, almost 30 percent of all trees in the Northeast are red maples. They appear throughout the Northeast, being one of the most adaptable trees. They can be found almost anywhere—from swamps to poor dry soils, and every condition in between. They can also grow at a wide range of elevations, from sea level to about 3,000 feet.

KEYS

- Opposite branching
- Red twigs, buds, flowers, and fall color
- Bull's-eyes in the bark
- Swamp maple

OPPOSITE BRANCHING

A tree with opposite branching has at least some of its branches coming off a larger branch directly opposite each other. **Figure 1.1** shows the difference between opposite branching and alternate branching.

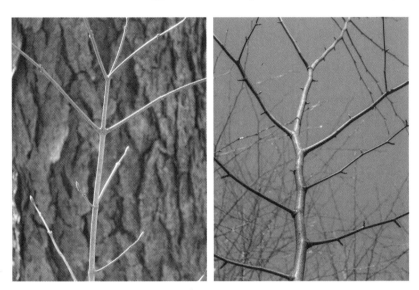

Figure 1.1 On the left is a red maple sapling showing opposite branching, on the right, a black birch showing alternate branching.

Only three trees that are commonly encountered in the forests of the Northeast have opposite branching: red maple, sugar maple, and ash. This means that if you see at least one pair of opposite branches (**Figure 1.2**), you know it is either a maple or an ash. Because ash branches are so unlike maple branches, it is easy to tell which one you are looking at (see Section 6, "How to tell a maple from an ash"). Both red maple and sugar maple have opposite branching. To learn how to differentiate them, see Section 3, "How to tell a red maple from a sugar maple."

Figure 1.2 Opposite branching maples. One pair of opposite branches is enough to establish that the tree is opposite branching.

RED TWIGS, BUDS, FLOWERS, AND FALL COLOR

There is something red about red maple year round—red twigs, red buds, red flowers, and, in the fall, red leaves. It is hard to see buds or twigs on a tall mature tree, so they are not much help in identifying it. On young trees or trees with new growth within reach, buds and twigs can be useful. Red maple leaves turn bright red in the fall, often before the leaves of other trees begin to turn. Then, very early in the spring, it is one of the first trees to flower, long before its leaves appear (Figure 1.3).

Figure 1.3 Red maple leaves turn red in the fall, and their flowers are red in the spring.

BULL'S-EYES IN THE BARK

If you see a tree with a pattern in its bark that looks like a bull's-eye, you can identify it as a red maple without a doubt (Figure 1.4). This unusual pattern in the bark is a trunk canker caused by a fungus. Even as a tree ages, the bull's-eye pattern persists.

Figure 1.4 The target-like patterns (formed by a trunk canker caused by a fungus) appear only on red maples and are identifiers.

SWAMP MAPLE

If you see opposite branching on a tree and it is growing in a swamp, lowland, or right next to water, then you know it is a red maple. Red maple is also known as swamp maple because it can thrive in wet areas (Figure 1.5), while sugar maple cannot tolerate these conditions.

Figure 1.5 Red maples do not mind getting their feet wet, while sugar maples do. Red maple leaves turn red before many other trees (bottom left).

I always feel at home where the sugar maple grows . . . glorious in autumn, a fountain of coolness in summer, sugar in its veins, gold in its foliage, warmth in its fibers, and health in it the year round.
—John Burroughs, *Under the Maples*

2 SUGAR MAPLE

Hard maple, rock maple

Sugar maple is the second most common tree in the Northeast. Its average life span is 300 years, and it can live up to 500 years. This means that many large mature trees populate our region. Some areas of the Northeastern forest are primarily composed of sugar maples. With the trees in close proximity, it is easy to tap them for their sap. An area of many maple trees being tapped for sap is called a "sugarbush." The sap is then transported to the sugarhouse where it is boiled down to make maple syrup and other maple-flavored products. In March, a popular dessert at church suppers in New England is "sugar-on-snow," made by boiling sap and then pouring it on a bowl full of hard-packed snow.

WHERE TO LOOK FOR SUGAR MAPLE

Sugar maple can be found throughout the Northeast. It has adapted to a variety of soil types, so it is not limited to specific conditions. It is also tolerant of shade, meaning it does not need direct sunlight to grow. Thus, it can start life even when overshadowed by more mature trees. It is one of the dominant species in mixed hardwood forests, so generally if you find one tree, you will find many throughout the forest. Unlike red maple, it does not tolerate wet roots, so it will not be found in swampy or boggy areas.

KEYS

- Opposite branching
- Sap lines
- Roadside rows
- Branches grow upward, oval shape
- Spiral growth

OPPOSITE BRANCHING

If you see at least one pair of opposite branches (**Figure 2.1**), it is either a maple or an ash (see Section 6, "How to tell maple from ash"). If you narrow it down and determine that it is a maple, then see Section 3, "How to tell red maple from sugar maple."

Figure 2.1 Maple saplings showing opposite branching.

SAP LINES

Maple syrup is most commonly made from the sap of the sugar maple, so wherever you see sap buckets—or, more often these days, plastic tubing running through the woods—you are seeing a grove of maple trees, which is called a "sugarbush" (**Figure 2.2**). The sap lines are under negative pressure, which causes the sap to be drawn from the trees and delivered to a sap house where it is collected and then boiled down into maple syrup.

Figure 2.2 A sugarbush with sap tubing under negative pressure.

ROADSIDE ROWS

Sap is gathered in the early spring when snow is generally still on the ground. In the old days, the sap was collected in buckets on the trees, and workmen would go around with a horse- or oxen-drawn sleigh with a big barrel on it to gather all the sap from the buckets. Needless to say, it was difficult to draw a sleigh through thick woods, so to make it easier to gather the sap, settlers planted sugar maples along the road (**Figure 2.3**). If you see trees planted in a row along a thoroughfare, old or new, look closely. Chances are good, especially in New England, that they are sugar maples.

Figure 2.3 Sugar maples were planted along roads to make it easier to gather and transport sap in the early spring, when snow is still on the ground.

BRANCHES GROW UPWARD, OVAL SHAPE

It may seem self-evident that branches grow upward, but not all of them do. Some trees actually have branches that grow downward, and other trees have branches that grow in all directions. The branches of open-grown sugar maples, however, do all grow upward in a classic oval form (Figure 2.4). The major limbs and branches both grow vertically with slender tips and form the distinctive oval shape. You will occasionally see a maple tree growing by itself in the middle of a field. Most likely an early farmer either planted it or left it when the land was cleared to provide a place to eat lunch and rest in its shadow when working in the field.

> That was a day of delight and wonder.
> While lying the shade of the maple trees under—
> He felt the soft breeze at its frolicksome play;
> He smelled the sweet odor of newly mown hay.
>
> —Thomas Dunn English, "Under the Trees"

Figure 2.4 Open-grown maple trees have a classic oval shape with branches that grow upward and become very slender at their ends.

SPIRAL GROWTH

Not all maples grow in spirals, but enough do that it is a secondary characteristic for identification (Figure 2.5). Some scientists speculate that this feature evolved to help the tree withstand high winds.

Figure 2.5 Sugar maples sometimes grow in a spiral pattern, unlike most other trees.

3 HOW TO TELL RED MAPLE FROM SUGAR MAPLE

It is not easy to tell red maple from sugar maple. As Chuck Wooster writes in *Northern Woodlands* magazine, "telling red maple from sugar maple can vex even seasoned botanists on occasion." That said, there are a number of keys that help distinguish the two maples.

KEYS

- Red maple found near water
- Bark differences
- Red vs. brown twigs and buds
- And the odds are . . .

RED MAPLE FOUND NEAR WATER

Red maple—or swamp maple—can tolerate having wet roots, so if you know a given tree is a maple because of opposite branching, and if it is growing in or near water or a wet area, it is a red maple.

BARK DIFFERENCES

Red maple is also known as soft maple, while sugar maple is also called hard maple. The "hard" in "hard maple" is sometimes reflected in the appearance of the tree's bark. A tight, hard-looking bark can be found on some sugar maples but not on red maples (**Figure 3.1**).

As a general rule, if you try to peel the bark of a red maple, you will find it comes off easily, but sugar maple bark is rigid and does not come off, even if it looks like it is peeling (**Figure 3.2**).

Bull's-eyes sometimes appear in red maple bark but never in sugar maples (**Figure 3.3**).

Figure 3.1 As shown in these photographs, some sugar maples have especially tight, hard-looking bark. This type of bark is not found on mature red maples.

Figure 3.2 Red maple bark peels off easily (left), while sugar maple bark resists peeling, even when it looks like it will come off (right).

Figure 3.3 Bull's-eyes found only on red maple.

RED VS. BROWN TWIGS AND BUDS

In the Introduction, I said that I would avoid using twigs and buds in identification because they are so hard to see or obtain when dealing with a mature tree. However, because it is sometimes difficult to distinguish between sugar and red maple, I have included them here.

If nothing else, they can be used to identify seedlings—which might provide a clue to the mature trees around them.

Red maple has red twigs and buds (and red leaves in the fall and red flowers in the spring). The leaves of sugar maple, on the other hand, generally turn yellow or golden in the fall, and sugar maples have brown twigs and buds (Figure 3.4).

Figure 3.4 Red maple showing red buds and twigs (left); sugar maple showing brown buds and twigs (right).

AND THE ODDS ARE . . .

In the forests of the Northeast, red maple is the most common of all deciduous trees. In fact, there are twice as many of them as the next most common, sugar maple. Thus, if you determine a tree is a maple and guess that it is a red maple, you will likely be right two out of three times.

Oh leave this barren spot to me!
Spare, woodman, spare the beechen tree!
—Thomas Campbell, "The Beech Tree's Petition"

4 BEECH

Beech can live for up to 400 years. In the Northeast, they reach their greatest size in the alluvial soils of Ohio. Beech nuts are highly nutritious and eaten by many types of wildlife. Bears climb beech trees to get at the nuts: Look for five parallel claw marks.

WHERE TO LOOK FOR BEECH

Beech trees can be found throughout the Northeast. Because they can tolerate shade, they can germinate even under the dark canopy of a mature forest. They can grow in a shaded wood until eventually they begin shading out other species themselves, resulting in what is called a "climax forest"—a forest that will remain as is until some outside force, such as storms, fire, or logging, destroys it. They are also sometimes planted as dooryard trees and, because of their low spreading branches, are a favorite for kids to climb.

KEYS

- Smooth silver-gray bark
- Found in groups
- Beech bark disease
- Leaves stay on all winter

SMOOTH SILVER-GRAY BARK

Beech is among a number of trees that can be identified almost with certainty by their bark alone. Beech bark is smooth and silver-gray throughout the tree's life (**Figure 4.1**).

Figure 4.1 The smooth bark of a beech tree, which can have hues of light gray, silver, and sometimes blue.

Because of the beech tree's smooth bark, it is very tempting for people to carve their initials or other artwork into it (**Figure 4.2**). Because beech is unable to heal itself, the carvings remain for the life of the tree. I once saw a tree with lovers' initials carved inside a heart and the date 1832.

Figure 4.2 Unfortunately, many people find carving in beech bark to be irresistible. In the lower left photograph, one can tell that the carving was made many years ago by the way it is expanding and blurring with the tree's growth.

FOUND IN GROUPS

In addition to reproducing by seeds, beech trees have roots that can produce shoots which grow up to become nearby trees. Thus, beech is often found in colonies sharing one root system (Figure 4.3).

Figure 4.3 Because beech can propagate by shoots from their root system, they are often found in colonies.

BEECH BARK DISEASE

Although the bark of a normal healthy beech tree is smooth, there is an epidemic of beech bark disease, occurring when the bark is penetrated by the beech scale insect, after which two different fungi invade the wound. A canker forms, and then cankers spread and are fatal to the tree (Figure 4.4). Trees that die from beech bark disease typically break off 10 to 15 feet above the ground (Figure 4.5).

Figure 4.4 Beech bark disease in various stages.

Figure 4.5 Trees that have died from beech bark disease tend to break off 10 to 15 feet above the ground.

LEAVES STAY ON ALL WINTER

After the leaves of most trees have fallen in the fall, it is easy to spot young beech trees because their leaves tend to stay on all winter (Figure 4.6).

Red oak leaves can also remain on the tree during winter. To tell them apart, see Section 11, "How to tell red oak from beech in the winter."

Figure 4.6 Beech leaves tend to stay on young trees throughout the winter.

The ash her purple drops forgivingly
And sadly, breaking not the general hush
—James Russell Lowell, "An Indian-Summer Reverie"

5 ASH

If you have ever held a baseball bat, chances are you have held ash. In fact, because of its strength and straight grain, many things you have held—tool handles, boat oars, even solid-body electric guitars—have been made of ash. Despite its usefulness, it is under siege from the emerald ash borer. This beetle, whose larvae feed on the inner bark, has spread throughout the region since it was introduced from Asia in 2002. There are treatments that can control it, but they are not a cure. One measure to prevent its spread is to refrain from transporting firewood beyond its source.

WHERE TO LOOK FOR ASH

Ash can be found throughout the Northeast on higher ground in mixed hardwood forests. They like full sun and deep soils.

KEYS

- Opposite branching
- Diamond-shaped bark
- Flower buds and flowers

OPPOSITE BRANCHING

Like maples, ash trees can be identified by opposite branching. Unlike maples, however, their branches are thick and somewhat stubby (**Figure 5.1**).

Figure 5.1 Like maples, ash trees have opposite branching, but their branches are shorter and thicker, and they tend to grow with a straight central trunk.

DIAMOND-SHAPED BARK

It is relatively easy to identify ash trees by their bark (**Figure 5.2**). It has furrows with sharp narrow ridges. The ridges merge in "V" shapes, creating a distinctive pattern that is usually described as diamond-shaped or as an "X" pattern.

Figure 5.2 Ash tree bark with its diamond-shaped furrowed bark.

FLOWER BUDS AND FLOWERS

If you are out between late winter and early spring, you may see the ash buds or purple blossoms Lowell refers to in his poem above. These are unique and confirm that you are looking at an ash tree (**Figure 5.3**).

Figure 5.3 Early in the spring, before leaves form, ashes bud out and flower in a very conspicuous manner.

6 HOW TO TELL MAPLE FROM ASH

KEYS

▪ Ash branches differ from maple branches

ASH BRANCHES DIFFER FROM MAPLE BRANCHES

Maples and ashes both have opposite branching, but there should be no confusion. Maples have long slender branches while ashes have shorter thicker branches, even to the extent that some people think they look like pitchforks or TV antennas. When the leaves are off, you can see more air through an ash than through a maple. Simply looking at the two trees should be enough to know whether you are looking at a maple or an ash (**Figure 6.1**).

Figure 6.1 Ash trees on the left, with short thick branches, compared with maple trees on the right, with long slender branches. You can see much more air through ash trees.

O had the monster seen those lily hands
Tremble like aspen-leaves, upon a lute.
—William Shakespeare, *Titus Andronicus*

7 ASPEN

Popple

There are two species of aspen in North America: quaking aspen and bigtooth aspen. Both are so similar (the major difference being their leaves) that even in much of the scientific literature they are referred to collectively as aspen and commonly as popple. Cottonwood is very closely related, but different enough to be discussed separately in Section 8, "Cottonwood."

WHERE TO LOOK FOR ASPEN

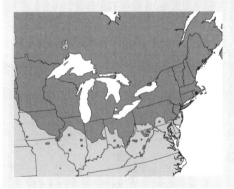

Aspen cannot tolerate shade, so, as can be seen in Figure 7.4, they will be found in meadows, along roadsides, or in clearings created by humans, windstorms, or forest fires. Geographically, aspen are widespread across the northern part of our region. They do not, however, grow at elevations much above 3,500 feet.

KEYS

- Two-toned bark
- Branch scars
- Grow in groves

TWO-TONED BARK

Once an aspen tree has begun to mature, its most distinctive characteristic is its two-toned bark. The rough bark of the lower trunk of the tree looks quite different from the smooth bark of the upper part of the trunk and branches (**Figure 7.1**).

Figure 7.1 The bark on the lower trunk of an aspen tree is rough, while the bark on the upper trunk and branches is lighter and smoother. This difference begins early in the tree's life, as shown in the photo on the lower right.

Figure 7.2 On the left is an example of an aspen with whitish bark, and on the right is one with greenish bark. Both show the horizontal black lines formed by merging lenticels.

The color of the upper bark of an aspen can range from white to gray to greenish. If it is white, it may at first appear to be a paper birch. One way to tell them apart is that paper birch bark peels and aspen bark does not.

As an aspen matures, its lower trunk grows darker and rougher. Because of the lower trunk's appearance, it may not be clear that it is an aspen, but if you look up into the branches and upper trunk, you will see that they are still smoother and lighter than the lower trunk.

The trunk features large obvious lenticels—pores that allow the tree's internal tissues to breathe. In aspen, they merge, forming raised black lines (Figure 7.2).

BRANCH SCARS

Aspens self-prune—that is, as the trees grow upward, their lower branches die and fall off. When they do, they leave a distinctive scar that can be used for identification (Figure 7.3). You can use your imagination to describe its shape . . . perhaps a bird on the wing?

Figure 7.3 Typical scars left as the lower branches of aspen die and fall off.

GROW IN GROVES

Aspen propagate by sending up multiple shoots from their root systems. This can result in a grove in which many aspen trees grow in close proximity (**Figure 7.4**). Aspen trees are fairly short-lived, from 40 to 150 years, but when the above-ground portion of the tree dies, the root system stays alive and continues to put up new shoots. Thus aspen can survive forest fires, and one root system can live for thousands of years. One such aspen community in Utah, called "Pando," is estimated to be eighty thousand years old.

Figure 7.4 A grove of aspen is actually a single organism. When the trees die, the roots do not. They continue to send up shoots that grow into new trees for many generations.

Perhaps you have noticed that even
in the very lightest breeze
you can hear the voice of the cottonwood tree
—Black Elk (1863–1950), medicine man of the Oglala Lakota (Sioux)

8 COTTONWOOD

Poplar

Cottonwood is the same genus, *populous*, as aspen, but differs from it in several ways. An obvious one is that a cottonwood can grow to be one of the largest of trees. It is not uncommon to find trees with diameters of five or six feet. They may well be the most massive trees around, especially in locations near water. Cottonwood gets its name from its white fuzzy seeds that float in the air and blanket the ground during the month of June. The seeds can be a nuisance and can also be dangerous, as they are extremely flammable.

WHERE TO LOOK FOR COTTONWOOD

Cottonwood is widespread and most often found in moist locations of every sort: river banks, pond edges, ditches, floodplains, and even swamps, where they may tolerate standing in water for short periods of time.

KEYS

- Deeply furrowed bark
- Branches at varying angles

DEEPLY FURROWED BARK

Cottonwood bark has furrows separated by flat ridges. On a mature tree, the ridges can be quite wide and long, in keeping with the tree's massive size. As it matures, the furrows become deeper (**Figure 8.1**). It differs from other trees with furrowed bark by being a light gray, rather than black or brown, and by the flatness of its ridges.

Figure 8.1 The light gray cottonwood bark grows progressively more furrowed as it ages, with the youngest at the top left and oldest at the bottom right.

BRANCHES AT VARYING ANGLES

While many trees grow with a regular, orderly arrangement of branches, cottonwoods do just the opposite; their branches go every which way at varying angles (**Figure 8.2**). Because the tree's wood is weak, branches often break in heavy storms.

Figure 8.2 The branches of cottonwood grow in a disorderly and unpredictable way.

> I frequently tramped eight or ten miles through the deepest snow to keep an appointment with a beech-tree, or a yellow birch, or an old acquaintance among the pines.
>
> —Henry David Thoreau, *Walden*

9 YELLOW BIRCH

Silver birch, swamp birch

Yellow birch is a handsome tree and the most valuable of the birches. It is slow-growing and long-lived. Its wood is strong and close-grained and is widely used for cabinetry, veneer, flooring, and furniture.

WHERE TO LOOK FOR YELLOW BIRCH

Yellow birch are found throughout the northern portions of our region and at higher elevations down through the Appalachian Mountains. They can tolerate some shade and some sun. They are aggressive in the sense that if a fallen tree leaves an opening in the forest, yellow birch are likely to start populating that opening. They can also grow in many different soil types and can be found mixed in with a variety of hardwoods or coniferous trees at higher elevations.

KEYS

- Yellow or silver curly bark
- Legs
- Scent

YELLOW OR SILVER CURLY BARK

If a tree is obviously yellow, especially one with horizontally peeling bark, it is a yellow birch. Unfortunately, there is a great deal of variation in the bark of yellow birches (**Figure 9.1**). It is usually sufficiently off-white that it will not be confused with paper birch bark, which is pure white (see Section 20, "Paper birch").

Figure 9.1 The color of young yellow birches can range from very light yellow, to yellow or golden, to silver-gray or bronze. The bark peels horizontally, and lenticels, appearing as horizontal lines, are prominent.

Figure 9.2 The bark of mature yellow birches. On the top are aging trees whose bark transitions to silver/gray. The specimen on the lower left is about 500 years old—it was found in a stand of old-growth hardwoods.

As yellow birch matures, its bark loses its colorful cast, becoming darker and more ragged. There is a certain shaggy look to old yellow birches that gives them an appearance of great character, one that I think makes them look like the granddads or old wise men of the forest (Figure 9.2). As with many other trees, such as aspen and sycamore, the bark on new branches higher up will still look like that of younger trees.

LEGS

Yellow birch aggressively seeds into forest clearings, and when it does, the new trees love to start life on the stumps or trunks of fallen trees (referred to as "nurse logs"). As they grow, their roots begin to reach for the ground. Years later, when the dead tree has completely decomposed, the yellow birch is left standing on legs (Figure 9.3). Some other trees do the same, but most often it is yellow birch—and it will certainly catch your eye as you walk through the woods.

Figure 9.3 Yellow birches on legs, each of which formed by first starting to grow on a nurse log, which eventually decomposed.

SCENT

There are several trees that can be identified by their smell. Yellow birch is one. If you scratch the bark or run your thumbnail down a bare twig, there will be a strong scent of wintergreen oil. Black birch has the same property.

A monk asked Chao-chou Ts'ung shen, "Has the oak tree
   Buddha nature?"
Chao-chou said, "Yes, it has."
The monk said, "When does the oak tree attain Buddhahood?"
Chao-chou said, "Wait until the great universe collapses."
The monk said, "When does the universe collapse?"
Chao-chou said, "Wait until the oak tree attains Buddhahood."
                    —Wumen Huikai, *The Gateless Barrier*

10 RED OAK

Northern red oak

There are various opinions as to why red oak is called "red": The name
is variously attributed to the color of the tree's leaves in the fall, the
color of its twigs, the pinkish color of its inner bark, and the cast of
lumber cut from it. It is one of the most valuable species in the forest
because of high demand for its wood. The larger the tree's diameter,
the more valuable it is, because wider boards, which command higher
prices, can be cut from it.

WHERE TO LOOK FOR RED OAK

Red oak can be found throughout
the Northeast, but it prefers the
warmer southern regions and
valleys. It tends to favor deep
soil. It is rare to find it above
elevations of 1,200 to 1,400
feet. Strangely, as shown on the
map, one should give up looking
for red oak in the heart of New
York's Adirondack Mountains—
there are virtually none to be
found there.

KEYS

- Commanding appearance, heavy limbs
- Ski-trail bark
- Leaves remain in winter
- Wintergreen underneath
- Coppice oaks

COMMANDING APPEARANCE, HEAVY LIMBS

> The monarch oak, the patriarch of the trees,
> Shoots rising up, and spreads by slow degrees.
> Three centuries he grows, and three he stays
> Supreme in state; and in three more decays.
>
> —John Dryden, "Palamon and Arcite"

Over the centuries, oak has come to be considered the imperial tree and the universal symbol for strength and steadfastness. To what does it owe this honor? Its commanding appearance reflects these qualities (**Figure 10.1**). One of the characteristics that contributes to its aura is how heavy its limbs are. Rather than quickly tapering like most trees, they project the same strength and weightiness as the trunk.

SKI-TRAIL BARK

It is likely that the stature of the tree and its heavy limbs will be enough to identify a red oak, but to eliminate any doubt, it can also be identified fairly easily by its hard and tight bark. There is never any shreddding or peeling. When young, the furrows are reddish. The ridges are smooth, sometimes so smooth that they reflect the light and appear white (**Figure 10.2**). The arrangement of the ridges and furrows running down the tree is often described as "ski trails."

Figure 10.1 Red oaks with their powerful trunks and massive branches.

Figure 10.2 The furrows of red oak bark have a reddish tinge. The ridges are flat. It is said that oak bark looks like ski trails.

As an oak tree ages, the red furrows tend to disappear, but the ridges continue to look like ski trails (Figure 10.3). (To differentiate red oak and white oak, see Section 13, "How to tell red oak from white oak.")

Figure 10.3 On mature red oaks, the ridges remain, but the red can no longer be seen in the furrows.

LEAVES REMAIN IN WINTER

In the fall, the nutrients in oak leaves return to the tree and its roots, resulting in leaves that are little more than cellulose. That makes them tough and leathery (and a poor choice for composting). Many stay attached to the tree through the winter, so if you see leaves on a tree after all have fallen from other trees, it could be an oak (**Figure 10.4**). The only other tree whose leaves tend to stay attached in the winter is beech (see Section 11, "How to tell red oak from beech in the winter").

As Robert Frost wrote in his poem "Reluctance": "The leaves are all dead on the ground / Save those that the oak is keeping."

Figure 10.4 Oak leaves can remain on the tree into and through the winter. On the lower right are leaves that have grown shiny and leathery as the season progresses.

WINTERGREEN UNDERNEATH

If snow has not covered the ground, another clue may lie under oak trees: wintergreen (**Figure 10.5**). Oak leaves on the ground are so thick and leathery that the roots of most plants cannot penetrate them to establish themselves. Wintergreen is the exception; its roots can pierce oak leaves. If you see wintergreen on the ground, look up. There will likely be an oak overhead.

Figure 10.5 Wintergreen and wintergreen berries growing in oak leaf cover.

COPPICE OAKS

Oaks are some of the most valuable trees in the forest, so some loggers, wanting to maximize their profits, cut the oaks first while bypassing other less-valuable species. Sprouts then grow from the oak stumps and, over the years, mature into multiple trees sharing the same base and root system. These oaks are referred to as "coppice oaks" (**Figure 10.6**). Other trees can do this, but because oaks tend to be harvested the most, they are the most likely to reappear as coppice trees.

Figure 10.6 Coppice oaks grown from the stumps of a previous generation of oaks.

11 HOW TO TELL RED OAK FROM BEECH IN THE WINTER

KEYS

- Dissimilar leaves

DISSIMILAR LEAVES

Red oaks and young beeches both hang on to some of their leaves all winter. However, it is easy to tell them apart, not only by the bark, but by the difference in their respective leaves' appearances (Figure 11.1). As beech trees mature, however, their leaves tend to fall, so if you see leaves high up in a mature tree, it is an oak.

Figure 11.1 Beech leaves, on the left, have a very different appearance than oak leaves, on the right. Beach leaves are oval in shape and generally light-colored. Red oak leaves have the usual lobes and valleys of oaks and are a leathery dark brown.

America has the grandest trees on earth—the largest, the oldest, and some of the most magnificent. Now, with Congressional passage and presidential signing of a historic bill, America has an official National Tree—the oak.

—Arbor Day Foundation, December 12, 2004

12 WHITE OAK

Stave oak

If oaks are known as the king of trees, white oaks have been called the king of kings. When grown in the open, the top grows broadly, with large branches extending out at wide angles. Its valuable wood has found many uses, including as staves for wooden barrels used to age whiskey and wine. As with many oaks, its acorns are an important food for wildlife. The largest trees are found in Delaware and on Maryland's eastern shore. White oaks have been known to live more than 500 years.

WHERE TO LOOK FOR WHITE OAK

As the map shows, white oak is widespread, but in the northern reaches it is likely to grow where lakes or the ocean tend to moderate the cold weather. It is a very versatile tree; it can be found on ridges, in valleys, in dry and moist habitats, and in soils that are acidic as well as alkaline. It is most often found in mature hardwood forests.

KEYS

- Light bark
- Bark broken vertically and horizontally
- Flared base

LIGHT BARK

White oak gets its name from the light color of both its wood and its bark. It grows in hardwood forests where its light color contrasts with the darker trees around it (Figure 12.1).

Figure 12.1 The light color of white oaks makes them stand out from the darker trees around them.

BARK BROKEN VERTICALLY AND HORIZONTALLY

White oak bark is broken vertically and horizontally into roughly rectangular shapes whose pattern has been described as checkerboarded (Figure 12.2).

Figure 12.2 White oak bark breaking vertically and horizontally into rectangles, sometimes called checkerboarding.

FLARED BASE

Although not true of every specimen, white oak trunks tend to flare out at the bottom, like a trumpet resting on its bell (Figure 12.3). Some other trees may do this as well, but it is typical enough of white oaks to be one key to identifying them.

Figure 12.3 Flared bases, typical of white oaks.

13 HOW TO TELL RED OAK FROM WHITE OAK

KEYS

- Bark character and color

BARK CHARACTER AND COLOR

There are more than 150 different kinds of oaks in North America, and many tree identification books include 40 or more. But only two are the most numerous and the most commonly found in mixed hardwood forests of the Northeast: red oak and white oak. There are two ways to tell them apart by their bark: Red oak bark is furrowed and dark, while white oak bark is broken into rectangles and is decidedly lighter. (**Figure 13.1**).

Figure 13.1 Each photo shows a red oak (left) and white oak (right) growing next to each other. Besides being whiter or lighter than red oak, white oak bark is broken up in a way some say resembles a checkerboard, while red oak bark is furrowed vertically into what look like ski trails.

School days, school days,
Dear old golden rule days.
'Readin' and 'ritin' and 'rithmetic,
Taught to the tune of a hick'ry stick.
　　　—"School Days," music by Gus Edwards, lyrics by Will D. Cobb

14 SHAGBARK HICKORY

Andrew Jackson, U.S. President and Major General during the War of 1812, was nicknamed "Old Hickory" because he was so tough. Hickory is denser, stiffer, and harder than either white oak or sugar maple. Because of its strength, it is used for tool handles and in sporting goods. Shagbark hickory is the most common hickory in the Northeast, and its nuts have been a staple food for both people and wildlife.

WHERE TO LOOK FOR SHAGBARK HICKORY

Shagbark hickory can grow in wet or dry areas, but it prefers well-drained soils. It can also be found on ledges. It is often associated with oaks, pines, and maples.

KEYS

- Shaggy bark
- May be found in woodland savannahs

SHAGGY BARK

It is no surprise that the most notable feature of the shagbark hickory is its shaggy bark (Figure 14.1). That alone is enough to identify the tree. Although young trees start off smooth, their bark soon begins to peel upward.

Figure 14.1 Shagbark hickory with its vertically peeling bark strips.

MAY BE FOUND IN WOODLAND SAVANNAHS

We think of savannahs as broad grassy plains, so a *woodland* savannah sounds like an oxymoron. What it refers to is a forest area that has nothing growing in the understory except grass (**Figure 14.2**). Oak, hophornbeam, and hickory are often associated with woodland savannahs.

Figure 14.2 Copses of shagbark can be found in woodland savannahs, where the forest floor is primarily grass.

The tulip-tree, high up,
Opened, in airs of June, her multitude
Of golden chalices to humming birds
And silken-winged insects of the sky.
                    —William Cullen Bryant, "The Fountain"

15 YELLOW POPLAR

Tulip tree, tulip poplar, whitewood, fiddle-tree

Yellow poplar is a beautiful tree that is also the tallest eastern hardwood, stretching as high as 150 feet or more with a trunk diameter of up to four feet. Water can rise from its roots to its top in an hour, and the tree can absorb a full ton of it on a summer day. It is a very valuable timber tree. It grows rapidly, but unlike other fast-growing trees, such as aspen and cottonwood, its wood remains strong. The common name "tulip tree" originated because of the tree's beautiful tulip-like flowers (the golden chalices to which Bryant refers above). The flowers also yield large quantities of nectar, making it a favored honey tree.

WHERE TO LOOK FOR YELLOW POPLAR

As the map shows, yellow poplar is not found west of Indiana, and it avoids the northern cold climes. It often grows at the edges of fields, in moist woodlands, and especially on downslopes where water drains. It can be found in virgin forests in the central and southern Appalachian Mountains.

KEYS

- Fruit cones on tree all winter
- Inverted "U" at branches

FRUIT CONES ON TREE ALL WINTER

The yellow poplar is commonly called the "tulip tree" because its flowers and fruits are shaped very much like a tulip. When the flowers are gone, the scales of the fruit cones remain on the tree throughout the winter. They too are tulip-shaped, making the tree easy to identify (**Figure 15.1**).

Figure 15.1 When winter comes, the tulip-shaped blossom leaves the scales of its fruit cone on the ends of small branches.

INVERTED U AT BRANCHES

Where branches meet the gray-green trunk, there is a dark inverted "U," a distinguishing mark of yellow poplar (**Figure 15.2**).

Figure 15.2 An inverted "U" appears where branches emerge from the trunk.

Displaying various hues of yellow, orange, bright red and purple—often on the same branch—[tupelo] foliage is a stand-out of the autumn season. Even the distinctive bark, which resembles alligator hide, adds visual and textural interest.

—Arbor Day Foundation

16 TUPELO

Black gum, swamp gum, sour gum, pepperidge tree

There are two commonly recognized varieties of tupelo: black tupelo and swamp tupelo. They can usually be identified by their different habitats: Black tupelo grows on the less organic soils of uplands, while swamp tupelo tends to grow on the heavy organic or clay soils of wet bottomlands. However, they can intermingle. Both are commonly referred to as "black gum." Here we refer primarily to the swamp variety.

WHERE TO LOOK FOR TUPELO

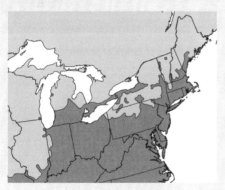

Tupelo can be found throughout the Northeast except in the northerly reaches. It grows best in full sun but will tolerate light shade. The swamp variety will be found in swamps, bogs, and moist areas at lower elevations.

KEYS

- Found in moist or swampy areas
- Alligator bark
- Crooked growth
- Broken tops

FOUND IN MOIST OR SWAMPY AREAS

The genus *Nyssa*, to which tupelo belongs, derives from Nysseides, the Greek water nymph. The common name, tupelo, comes from *topilwa*, a Creek Indian word meaning "swamp tree." Thus it is not surprising that we tend to find tupelo in moist or swampy areas (**Figure 16.1**).

Figure 16.1 Tupelo is often found growing in moist areas or in swamps.

ALLIGATOR BARK

The bark of young tupelo begins to furrow vertically (**Figure 16.2**). It then continues with deepening furrows and higher ridges, which begin breaking horizontally. A mature tree can have very deep furrows and fissures. The bark is often described as looking like the back of an alligator.

A strange configuration can sometimes be observed. The tree will show the deeply furrowed bark on one side and a smoother bark on the other (**Figure 16.3**). One theory is that this occurs when the tree is leaning, causing snow and ice to form on the upper side, which, in turn, causes the large furrows of bark to slough off with freezing and thawing.

Figure 16.2 The alligator bark of black tupelo in its growth stages, with the youngest shown in the upper left and the most mature in the lower right.

TUPELO

83

Figure 16.3 Some trees show deeply furrowed bark on one side and smoother bark on the other.

CROOKED GROWTH

You may have heard the poem "There was a crooked man" when you were a child. Well, with tupelo, there was a crooked tree. The branches and trunk can be very crooked or wavy (**Figure 16.4**). Dooryard trees must often be pruned to maintain a normal form.

Figure 16.4 The crooked trunks and branches of tupelo. Some of the trees in this swamp have been dated to be as old as 400 years.

BROKEN TOPS

When most deciduous trees get heart rot (decay in the center of the tree), it generally appears first at the bottom of the tree and works its way up the trunk. The opposite happens with tupelo; its heart rot begins at the top of the tree. That could be so that in a high wind, the top breaks off instead of the tree being blown over, a concern since it is only weakly rooted in wet soil (Figure 16.5).

Figure 16.5 The tops of tupelos may break off in a high wind.

Thou lookest on the lime-leaf,
Thou a heart's form will discover;
Therefore are the lindens ever
Chosen seats of each fond lover.

—Heinrich Heine, *Book of Songs*

17 BASSWOOD

Linden, bee-tree

Basswood is a fast-growing tree whose wood is prized by woodcarvers for its softness and its fine, almost invisible grain. It is also called "bee-tree" because of the sweet nectar in its flowers, which makes a delicious honey.

WHERE TO LOOK FOR BASSWOOD

Basswood can be found in mixed hardwood stands throughout the Northeast. It is fast-growing and is planted occasionally as a dooryard tree. In the East it is also planted as an urban tree.

KEYS

- Light gray, vertically cracked bark
- Hollow sound when struck

LIGHT GRAY, VERTICALLY CRACKED BARK

Although a description of basswood bark may sound like many other trees, it is different enough to make it fairly easy to recognize—in part because its gray bark is generally lighter than other trees around. When young, it is light gray with vertical cracks. As it matures it begins to form shallow furrows with long flat ridges (Figure 17.1). The flat

Figure 17.1 Basswood bark starts off light gray with vertical cracks (top left). Then the cracks start forming furrows with flat ridges. The furrows are narrow while the flat ridges are wide, giving the tree the appearance of being smooth. The gray bark is lighter than that of many other trees.

ridges are wide while the furrows are very narrow. This gives the tree the overall impression of being round and smooth with narrow vertical cracks. It has been said that it looks like the bark of an ash tree that has been sanded down.

HOLLOW SOUND WHEN STRUCK

Can you identify a tree by sound? Believe it or not, with basswood you can. If you think you have found one because of the bark, pick up a stick or stone and hit the tree hard. If it is basswood, it will sound hollow.

Even if I knew that tomorrow the world would go to pieces, I would still plant my apple tree.

—Attributed to Martin Luther

18 APPLE

The apples we are used to eating originated in the Himalayas and then made their way west across the Caucuses to the Mediterranean and from there to the United States. Although apple is a domesticated tree, it can occasionally be found in forests, especially in New England. When found, it is a sign that a settler or family lived there long ago and planted a dooryard tree. Look at the area around the tree. Is there a cellar hole?

WHERE TO LOOK FOR APPLE TREES

Apples were first brought to North America in the 1600s, and soon colonists were planting orchards. Apple trees and their many varieties can be found virtually everywhere. Johnny Appleseed (John Chapman) introduced apple trees from Ontario to northern West Virginia. Apples provide a great source of nourishment for deer and other mammals, which spread the seeds through their digestive tracts.

KEYS

- Apples
- Winter bud on spur
- Tend to have suckers and waterspouts
- Somewhat shaggy bark

APPLES

Apples, it may seem obvious to say, indicate an apple tree, and in some cases they remain on the branches well into winter (**Figure 18.1**).

Figure 18.1 Apples can remain on the branch long after the leaves have fallen. On the lower right are crab apples, the only indigenous American apple.

WINTER BUD ON SPUR

A distinctive feature of apple trees is that they have short spurs with buds on them (Figure 18.2). The spurs can be very sharp. The branches are thick.

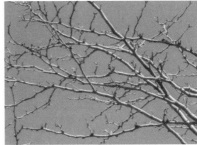

Figure 18.2 Short stumpy spurs with buds on them are a distinctive feature of apple trees. The spurs can be sharp.

TEND TO HAVE SUCKERS AND WATERSPOUTS

Mature apple trees tend have suckers (fast-growing vertical shoots that rob the tree of energy) growing from their roots and waterspouts (vertical shoots that grow from the trunk or branches) (Figure 18.3).

Figure 18.3 Apple waterspouts growing straight up from the trunk (left) and suckers, shoots growing from the base of the tree or its roots (right).

SOMEWHAT SHAGGY BARK

Apple tree bark is quite shaggy. It looks as though if you were to run your hand down it, pieces would just flake off—and they do (**Figure 18.4**).

Figure 18.4 Apple trees have a shaggy appearance. If you study a few of them, it becomes relatively easy to spot them only by their bark.

The ancient Egyptians used willow bark as a remedy for aches and pain. They didn't know that what was reducing body temperature and inflammation was the salicylic acid (aspirin) in the leaves and bark.

—Diarmuid Jeffreys, *Aspirin: The Remarkable Story of a Wonder Drug*

19 WILLOW

Willows are symbolic of sorrow. Their likeness is carved on many an old slate gravestone (**Figure 19.1**). In Shakespeare's *Othello*, Desdemona laments her lost love in the "Willow Song." Although it is an attractive tree, those who plant one in their front yard often come to regret their choice because willow branches are brittle and easily break off in snow or wind, the tree's water-seeking roots can clog sewer lines, and it has a short life. Willows are in the same family as Cottonwoods, and their bark is quite similar.

Figure 19.1 The willow was a common motif on slate gravestones from the late 1700s through the early 1800s.

WHERE TO LOOK FOR WILLOW

Willows in the wild occur naturally in wetlands and on stream banks, where they grow especially well. Their dense mat of roots reduces erosion and helps control floods.

KEYS

- Hanging branchlets

HANGING BRANCHLETS

Willows are recognizable, even from afar, by their large crowns with branchlets that hang down (the branchlets of weeping willows can sweep the ground). The leaves are long and slender, and the branchlets are light brown or yellow brown (Figure 19.2).

Figure 19.2 Long hanging branchlets and, in warm weather, long slender leaves, make it easy to spot willow trees.

Nothing will be left white but here a birch,
And there a clump of houses with a church.
                              —Robert Frost, "The Onset"

20 PAPER BIRCH

White birch, canoe birch

Paper birch is near and dear to almost everyone's heart, whether planted in a yard, pictured in scenes on Christmas cards, or chopped up into a few decorative logs in an unused fireplace. It may appear to be the easiest tree to identify, however it can be confused with gray birch, some silvery yellow birches, and even young aspen and sycamores. The reason we call it *paper birch* rather than *white birch* is to avoid confusion with gray birch, which is also white (see Section 22, "How to tell paper birch from gray birch").

WHERE TO LOOK FOR PAPER BIRCH

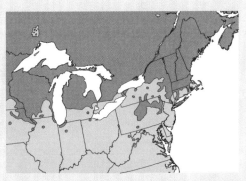

Paper birch grows rapidly to a medium size. It can be found in many growing conditions throughout a large but northern range in mixed hardwood and conifer forests, and it may be the first tree species to seed into open areas, where they can sometimes be found in pure stands. It is one of a few trees that can grow at high elevations, and it can be found near the tree line on higher mountains.

KEYS

- White curly bark
- Early adapter and short-lived

WHITE CURLY BARK

One hallmark of paper birch is its bark's tendency to curl horizontally (**Figure 20.1**).

Figure 20.1 Young paper birch is white with generally small narrow curls.

As birches mature, larger curls appear and the lenticels may grow larger until they appear as black lines (Figure 20.2). Lenticels are small holes in the bark through which a tree breathes. They can form in rows appearing as lines.

Figure 20.2 The curls of bark grow larger as paper birch matures and the lenticels form black lines.

As a paper birch nears full maturity, it may be a little more difficult to identify by its bark. The bark can grow gray and darker (**Figure 20.3**). However, as an aid to identification, look up: The new growth on the tree—higher branches and new branches and twigs—will display the same light bark as a younger tree.

Figure 20.3 Fully mature paper birch with bark turning darker and lenticels growing to give it a horizontally striped appearance.

EARLY ADAPTER AND SHORT-LIVED

Sometimes in a forest, mature trees can be felled by windstorms, fire, or logging. This allows the sun to dry out the soil. The same is true of open areas like meadows. Paper birch is one of the species that can thrive under these conditions. As a result, foresters call it an "early adapter" (Figure 20.4).

Figure 20.4 Paper birches seeding in and growing in meadows or areas of disturbance (e.g., fires, storms, logging)—sometimes in groves or pure stands.

After establishing themselves, birches start shading the ground, resulting in moister soil. Soon other species begin to take root and grow up under the birch until eventually they outgrow and begin shading it. When this happens, the birch, which has a short lifespan—about 75 years—will begin to die off (Figures 20.5 and 20.6).

Figure 20.5 Standing dead paper birch.

Figure 20.6 Having been superseded by other, more shade-tolerant species, paper birch dies and falls to the ground in a mature forest.

The one thing I haven't done is to use white or gray birch for posts. . . . I had read most of Robert Frost and could quote from "Home Burial": "Three foggy mornings and one rainy day / Will rot the best birch fence a man can build."

—Noel Perrin, *First Person Rural: Essays of a Sometime Farmer*

21 GRAY BIRCH

Gray birch grows relatively rapidly, but it does not attain great height or girth. Its lifespan is about 30 years. It is often planted as a dooryard tree in preference to paper birch because it tolerates a greater range of heat and humidity and is more resistant to several insect species.

WHERE TO LOOK FOR GRAY BIRCH

Gray birch is confined to the more easterly portion of the Northeast. It is an early adapter, meaning it is one of the first trees to grow in a clearing. It does well in both dry and moist soil, though it is fairly short-lived. Often it is the only tree that colonizes mine tailings, gravel pits, quarries, and other such disturbed sites, so if you see white trees in these locations, it is most likely gray birch.

KEYS

- Black triangle
- Chalky

BLACK TRIANGLES

Where gray birch branches meet the trunk, a distinctive black triangle forms (Figure 21.1).

Figure 21.1 At the base of gray birch branches, black triangles form.

CHALKY

Although the bark of gray birch is similar to that of paper birch, you can generally tell the difference between them by rubbing your fingers down the bark. Nothing happens with paper birch, but gray birch bark can have a white chalky substance that easily rubs off on your fingers (**Figure 21.2**).

Figure 21.2 When you rub your fingers on gray birch bark, a white chalky substance can easily rub off.

KEYS

- Gray birch: no peeling
- Gray birch: chalky
- Black triangle vs. inverted "V"

GRAY BIRCH: NO PEELING

Gray birch is not nearly as common as paper birch and can be easily mistaken for it. One way to tell them apart is that paper birch exfoliates—that is, its bark curls horizontally away from the tree—while gray birch bark does not peel at all (**Figure 22.1**).

Figure 22.1 Paper birch, on the left, peels and curls, while gray birch, on the right, does not.

GRAY BIRCH: CHALKY

White birch bark is hard and smooth to the touch. Gray birch, on the other hand, can have a chalky feel to it with some white "chalk" rubbing off (see **Figure 21.2**).

BLACK TRIANGLE VS. INVERTED "V"

Where the branches of a gray birch meet the trunk, there is a prominent black triangle. On a paper birch, the corresponding shape is that of an inverted "V" (**Figure 22.2**).

Figure 22.2 Gray birch (left) with its black triangle contrasts with paper birch (right) with its inverted "V."

On making birch beer: Tap the tree as the sugar maple is tapped, in spring when the sap is rising and the buds are just swelling; jug the sap and throw in a handful of shelled corn, and natural fermentation will finish the job for you.

—Donald Culross Peattie, *A Natural History of Trees of Eastern and Central North America*

23 BLACK BIRCH

Sweet birch, cherry birch, mahogany birch

Black birch was originally prized as a source of wintergreen oil (giving it its name "sweet birch"), and forests of black birch were decimated. Distillers then attacked saplings, further endangering the species. It took 100 saplings to make one quart of oil. Wintergreen oil contains methyl salicylate (the natural form of aspirin), which accounts for its most common use in the past as an analgesic to relieve the pain of such conditions as arthritis, rheumatism, sore throats, and many others. Luckily, a synthetic substitute was found, and today, black birches have made a comeback. The unusual alternative name "mahogany birch" comes from the fact that its wood darkens and looks like mahogany, for which it has become an inexpensive substitute.

WHERE TO LOOK FOR BLACK BIRCH

Black birch can be found in the northern hardwood forest, along with sugar maple, oak, yellow birch, beech, and ash. Black birch tends not to grow above 1,800 feet in elevation.

KEYS

- Black bark with lenticels
- Catkins in fall
- Wintergreen scent

BLACK BARK WITH LENTICELS

Unsurprisingly, black birch bark is dark gray or black in color. Like the other birches, it has lenticels, which form obvious, slightly raised horizontal lines. Even when the tree is old and there are only fragments of its outer bark left, the lenticel lines are still visible (Figure 23.1).

Figure 23.1 From the top left to bottom right, these photographs illustrate the evolution of black birch bark as a tree matures. However, the lenticel lines remain throughout.

As a young tree, the bark is smooth. As it ages, vertical fractures begin to appear. These fractures grow larger and larger as the tree grows older, and they may result in large plates of bark (potentially the largest of any tree) pulling away from the tree horizontally. Ultimately, the bark may break up horizontally as well. Black birch bark does not peel the way the bark of yellow birch or paper birch does.

CATKINS IN FALL

The male flowers of black birches are called catkins (Figure 23.2). They are found at the end of twigs, they are yellowish-green, and they can be three to four inches long. They form in late summer or autumn on mature trees older than about 40 years and are present all winter. They tend to form in the new growth at the top of the tree.

Figure 23.2 Catkins form in the fall and remain on the tree all winter.

WINTERGREEN SCENT

Like yellow birch, black birch has a strong scent of wintergreen when you scratch the bark of a twig or crush the leaves, hence the common name "sweet birch." Birch beer was once made from the tree, as was a tea from its twigs. In the 1800s, oil of wintergreen was extracted from birch bark, but today the flavor is produced artificially.

River birch is the most beautiful of American trees.
—Prince Maximilian (1832–67), Emperor of Mexico

24 RIVER BIRCH

Many people agree with Prince Maximilian that river birch is a beautiful tree with its color and drooping branches. As a result, it has been widely used in landscaping.

WHERE TO LOOK FOR RIVER BIRCH

River birch tends to natively populate the southern part of our region, but because it is such a handsome tree, it has been widely planted in more northerly areas as an ornamental.

KEYS

- Orange-tinged bark

ORANGE-TINGED BARK

A river birch's form, branching, and leaves are similar to paper birch, but its bark sets it apart. It peels like paper birch bark, but its curls are thinner and it has a distinct orange tint (**Figure 24.1**).

Figure 24.1 River birch bark curls like paper birch but with thinner curls and a light-orange color.

I can't tell a lie, Pa; you know I can't tell a lie. I did cut the cherry tree with my hatchet.

—George Washington

25 BLACK CHERRY

Wild cherry

Black cherry trees are popular for many reasons: humans prize cherry wood for use in cabinetry and flooring; animals and a large number of birds use its small cherries as a food source; and a number of moths, including tent caterpillars and butterflies, use cherry trees for shelter.

WHERE TO LOOK FOR BLACK CHERRY

Black cherry is found throughout the Northeast in hardwood forests. It is intolerant of shade, so it starts its life in full sunlight. It does not like overly moist soils. It can also be found along roadways as a result of seeds that arrive in the droppings of birds sitting overhead on telephone wires.

KEYS

- Burnt potato chip bark

BURNT POTATO CHIP BARK

Black cherry is very easy to identify. You only need to know that it looks as if burnt potato chips were glued all over its trunk (Figure 25.1). No other tree looks quite like it.

Figure 25.1 Black cherry bark looks like burnt potato chips glued to the tree.

26 HOW TO TELL BLACK CHERRY FROM BLACK BIRCH

KEYS

- Dissimilar bark

DISSIMILAR BARK

For some reason, perhaps because both their names contain the word "black" or because the bark of each is dark, many people confuse black cherry and black birch. However, one glance at their different barks and it becomes clear which is which (**Figure 26.1**). Black cherry bark looks like burnt potato chips. Black birch bark is black with horizontal lines.

Figure 26.1 Black cherry bark, on the left, looks like burnt potato chips, while young black birch bark, on the right, is smooth with horizontal lines in it.

However, as black birch ages, its bark breaks into horizontal plates and is a little more similar to black cherry. Nonetheless, the horizontal lines of lenticels are still present and indicate that it is birch and not cherry (Figure 26.2).

Figure 26.2 The mature black birch on the right looks a little more similar to the black cherry on the left than the younger tree in Figure 26.1, but the horizontal lines of lenticels in the black birch bark and the way it breaks up into vertical plates distinguish it.

Thickets of pin cherry saplings that sprout straight up in sunny locations burst into blossom in early spring, adding unexpected beauty to the most mundane and neglected landscapes.

—Anne Krantz, University of New Hampshire
Tree Steward and Master Gardener

27 PIN CHERRY

Fire cherry, bird cherry, red cherry

Pin cherry is the poor cousin of the black cherry. While black cherry is a stately tree with great value as timber, pin cherry is much smaller, and its wood is soft and of little commercial value. It tends to establish itself after a fire (hence "fire cherry"). Its shade protects seedlings of slower-growing species, and it then dies off as they overtop it.

WHERE TO LOOK FOR PIN CHERRY

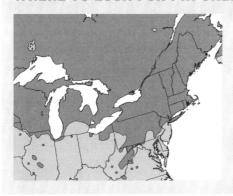

Pin cherry is widely distributed through the more northerly areas of our region and at the higher elevations in the Appalachian Mountains. It is a short-lived tree that prefers full sun. It often comes up in clearings, meadows, and areas that have burned over.

KEYS

■ Large rough lenticels

LARGE ROUGH LENTICELS

We have spoken of lenticels, especially in connection with the birches. Lenticels, which form lines in the bark, are small holes through which trees breathe. The pin cherry can be identified by its large coarse lenticels (Figure 27.1). Rather than appearing as lines within the bark, they bulge out and can easily be felt if you run your hand down the tree.

Figure 27.1 The lenticels of the pin cherry are large and clearly raised from the surrounding bark.

Striped maples are singularly beautiful trees. They are among the most shade tolerant of all trees in the Northeast. . . . Careful siting makes these beautiful trees garden-worthy in shady locations with cool moist soils; and elsewhere, striped maples are worth searching for, to admire in their forest homes.

—Pamela Johnson, Wild Seed Project

28 STRIPED MAPLE

Goosefoot maple, moosewood, whistlewood

Striped maple is a small understory tree that can tolerate shade and is often found along hiking trails. Like other maples, it has opposite branching. It is called "whistlewood" because slip-bark whistles can easily be made from it in the spring. It is called "goosefoot" maple after the shape of its leaves. And Boy Scouts will tell you it is called "camper toilet paper" for its large, strong, soft leaves.

WHERE TO LOOK FOR STRIPED MAPLE

The range of striped maple roughly follows the Appalachian Mountains, with a presence in northern Michigan and its Upper Peninsula. The tree can tolerate deep shade. The largest are only 20 or 30 feet tall. It can survive decades as a shrub. It is often present along hiking trails.

KEYS

- Strongly striped bark
- Bark rubbed off by deer and moose

STRONGLY STRIPED BARK

Striped maple lives up to its name. Its bark features strong vertical stripes, most often green and black, but it can also show white and silver effects (**Figure 28.1**). A certain identification can be made on the basis of these stripes.

Figure 28.1 Striped maple bark is aptly named.

BARK RUBBED OFF BY DEER AND MOOSE

In the late summer or fall, deer and moose rub their newly acquired antlers against trees to remove the velvet, with striped maple a frequently favored choice (Figure 28.2). This explains why it is sometimes called "moosewood."

Figure 28.2 Deer and moose like to use striped maple to rub the velvet off their new antlers.

Birds singing in the sycamore trees
Dream a little dream of me
—"Dream a Little Dream of Me," lyrics by Gus Kahn

29 SYCAMORE

Planetree, buttonwood, buttonball

The sycamore, one of the largest deciduous trees, is fairly common. They make a good shade tree because of their attractive bark and spreading dense crown. Sycamore is a fast-growing tree, and as the trunk expands, the rigid outer bark splits and peels, giving it its one-of-a-kind appearance.

WHERE TO LOOK FOR SYCAMORE

Sycamore shies away from the cold and is found in the more southerly areas of the Northeast or near bodies of water that temper the weather. Look along rivers and streams.

KEYS

- Camouflage-like peeling bark
- Tends to grow near water
- Massive

CAMOUFLAGE-LIKE PEELING BARK

Sycamore bark is unmistakable. Its unusual bark is multi-colored and suggestive of camouflage. The bark also has a tendency to peel (**Figure 29.1**).

Figure 29.1 Sycamore bark resembles camouflage and peels profusely.

Like many trees, as sycamore matures, the trunk darkens and loses youthful coloring. Look up at the newer growth at the top of the tree, however, and you will see the same characteristics as you would on the trunk of a younger tree (**Figure 29.2**).

Figure 29.2 The upper branches of these mature sycamores present the same camouflage bark as the lower trunks of younger trees.

TENDS TO GROW NEAR WATER

Sycamores love running water and are often found along streams and rivers (Figure 29.3).

Figure 29.3 Sycamores love to grow along rivers and streams.

MASSIVE

Sycamore can grow to be a massive tree, especially in Ohio and along the Mississippi river basin. The tree on the left in **Figure 29.4** is a sycamore in Sunderland, Massachusetts. It is 114 feet tall and 24.7 feet in girth. A plaque there reads: "The National Arborist Association and the International Society of Arboriculture jointly recognize this significant tree in this bicentennial year as having lived here at the time of the signing of our Constitution."

Figure 29.4 Sycamores can grow very large, such as the historic sycamore in Sunderland, Massachusetts (on the left), and others, such as the one on the right.

I'm that same David Crockett, fresh from the backwoods, half horse, half alligator, a little touched with the snapping turtle; can wade the Mississippi, leap the Ohio, ride upon a streak of lightening, and slip without a scratch down a honey locust.

—Attributed to Davy Crockett

30 BLACK LOCUST

Common locust, yellow locust

The honey locust Davy Crockett refers to above is a close relative of the black locust, a significant difference being that it has much longer thorns.

Locust can send a taproot down as deep as 20 feet. In the colonial days, an area of Connecticut was found to have bedrock about five feet down with locust growing above it. The locust taproot would hit the bedrock and turn 90 degrees. These right angle root bends were used as brackets to attach the decking of sailing ships to the hull.

WHERE TO LOOK FOR BLACK LOCUST

The map shows where black locust naturally appears. However, it has been widely planted and can be found throughout much of the Northeast. It grows on a wide range of sites but prefers moist, rich limestone soils.

KEYS

- Deep furrows, narrow ridges
- Scary-looking tree
- Along roads
- Propagation by rootstocks (rhizomes)

DEEP FURROWS, NARROW RIDGES

The bark of the black locust is its primary identifying feature. Its furrows are so deep and its ridges so narrow that it is hard to mistake it for another tree (Figure 30.1).

Figure 30.1 Typical examples of deeply furrowed black locust bark.

SCARY-LOOKING TREE

I think black locust trees look very much like the trees that appear in scary Halloween illustrations and in haunted house horror movies. Its tall narrow presence and curved "arms" reaching out give it its sinister appearance (Figure 30.2). Note that there are no straight branches.

Figure 30.2 Black locust can have a scary, sinister look.

ALONG ROADS

In areas where black locust was not native, pioneers and farmers planted it because its wood is so rot-resistant, which made for long-lasting fence posts. It was often planted along roads or near buildings (**Figure 30.3**). Sugar maple was planted along roads as well, but they are such different trees that it should be obvious which is which.

Figure 30.3 Black locust planted along roads.

PROPAGATION BY ROOTSTOCKS (RHIZOMES)

Locust can propagate by underground rhizomes, that is, a type of root that grows horizontally and sprouts new shoots that grow upward. The rhizomes of one black locust can spread as far as 20 feet. Thus, there are often groves or colonies of black locust, with many trees growing in one area from the same root system (Figure 30.4).

Figure 30.4 Black locust groves created by rhizomes.

Murugan swung his axe solidly at the tree. It was a species of ironwood and did honor to its name. The blunt edge of the axe slipped impotently off its bark.

—Aviott John, *The Ironwood Poacher and Other Stories*

31 HORNBEAM

Ironwood, blue beech, musclewood, water beech

Hornbeam and hophornbeam sound like related trees; they are not. To make matters worse, both trees are frequently called by the same common name, "ironwood" (see Section 33, "Ironwood"). To avoid confusion, one should discard the term "ironwood" and either use another common name or be very careful to make a distinction between hornbeam and hophornbeam.

WHERE TO LOOK FOR HORNBEAM

Hornbeam is a small tree that is often found in the understory. It likes wet but not saturated soils and has adapted to many conditions. It is called "water beech" because it can often be found in lowlands or along streams and rivers.

KEYS

- Bluish, muscled bark

BLUISH, MUSCLED BARK

The common name "blue beech" derives from the fact that hornbeam's bark is smooth and gray, similar to a beech but with a bluish cast; it is called "musclewood" because of its fluted appearance, which resembles a flexed muscle. Hornbeam can be identified by its bark and form alone (Figure 31.1).

Figure 31.1 Hornbeam whose muscle-like appearance gave rise to its common name "musclewood"; its bluish beech-like appearance gave rise to its common name "blue beech."

The hophornbeam might be considered the rough-and-tumble cousin of the more delicate-looking birch trees that they're related to.

—*Tree Link News*, Washington State Department of Natural Resources

32 HOPHORNBEAM

Ironwood, hardhack, leverwood

Hornbeam and hophornbeam are both commonly called "ironwood" because of the hardness and strength of their wood (see Section 33, "Ironwood"). "Leverwood," one common alternative name for hophornbeam, attests to the tree's strength when used by early settlers as a lever to move large stones as they cleared land and built stone walls. The "hop" in its name refers to the similarity between its fruits and the look and structure of hops.

WHERE TO LOOK FOR HOPHORNBEAM

Hophornbeam is adapted to a great variety of landscapes. It thrives in a wide range of soil types and pH levels, wet and dry conditions, and full sun or part shade. It is sometimes found in woodland savannahs, where grass grows with little or no understory (see Figure 14.2).

KEYS

- Shreddy bark

SHREDDY BARK

Hophornbeam trees are usually small, but on occasion, large examples stand out. Its gray to reddish-brown bark looks like is has been vertically shredded, making it easy to recognize (Figure 32.1).

Figure 32.1 Hophornbeam bark shreds in a narrow vertical pattern.

33 IRONWOOD

Around the world, there are more than thirty species of trees that are commonly called "ironwood" because of their strength. In the Northeast, two trees—both featuring wood that is, in fact, very hard, heavy, and strong—are commonly called "ironwood," causing confusion over their identification, despite their having radically different bark. The problem is compounded because of the similarity of their common names: "hornbeam" and "hophornbeam."

Here are both "ironwood" trees with the names that can be used to differentiate them (**Figure 33.1**).

Carpinus caroliniana
Hornbeam
Blue beech
Musclewood
Water beech

Ostrya virginiana
Hophornbeam
Leverwood

Figure 33.1 Differentiating the two trees commonly known as "ironwood."

There rises the moon, broad and tranquil, through the branches of a walnut tree on a hill opposite.

—Henry Wadsworth Longfellow, Letter to Charles Sumner, 1832

34 BLACK WALNUT

Mature specimens that have grown slowly and have at least eight feet of clear trunk—no branches and no blemishes—can command thousands to tens of thousands of dollars as veneer trees. However, because the veneer blades that slice a rotating log very thinly are expensive, the log cannot have any old bullets or fence wire or clothesline brackets buried in the wood. Trees may be x-rayed before purchase.

Its nuts are highly prized by squirrels. In one experiment, 420 walnuts were buried. Squirrels found and dug up 419 of them. People also prize them for their flavor, which is far more intense than that of regular (Carpathian) walnuts. Black walnut cake and ice cream are American favorites. Even walnut shells are put to good use. They are ground up into a powder and used in such applications as fine polishing and to clean airport runway lights.

WHERE TO LOOK FOR BLACK WALNUT

Black walnut is a fair-weather tree, avoiding the colder climes where there is heavy snowfall. It does appear in pockets in the upper Northeast, usually limited to areas near bodies of water (for instance, around the Finger Lakes in New York state) where the weather is a little milder. It is also farmed for its valuable wood and nuts.

KEYS

- Nuts
- Chambered pith
- Diamond pattern in bark
- Curving branches

NUTS

Black walnuts are prized for their flavor but perhaps cursed for how difficult it is to get to the nut-meat. First the outer husk has to be removed, which stains everything it touches. (To avoid staining, some people put black walnuts in the driveway and drive their cars back and forth over them.) Then, the thick heavy shell must be cracked. Finally, the nut-meats must be picked out of the intricate shell chambers. The large distinctive nuts can remain on the tree into autumn (**Figure 34.1**) after which they fall and litter the ground.

Figure 34.1 Black walnuts on a tree in the fall, and dried nuts ready for cracking and using in many different baked goods.

CHAMBERED PITH

Black walnut branches are often brittle, and I've been able to find twigs and branches on the ground under almost every tree. If you shave a twig down to its center—the pith—you will discover that it is made up of a row of chambers (**Figure 34.2**). With the exception of its close relative, the butternut tree, this alone is the basis for a positive identification.

 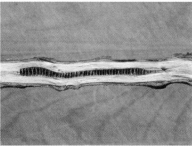

Figure 34.2 Chambered pith in a black walnut twig.

DIAMOND PATTERN IN BARK

When black walnut trees are young, the brown or gray bark displays wide flat ridges in a diamond-like pattern that is wider than ash bark ridges. As it ages, the ridges tend to break up (**Figure 34.3**) but still maintain their diamond-like pattern.

Figure 34.3 At the top left is a young black walnut. As trees mature, the wide flat ridges start breaking up. The tree on the lower right is around 150 years old.

CURVING BRANCHES

If a tree has straight limbs, it is not a black walnut. Black walnut limbs tend to curve and do not grow in a regular form (Figure 34.4).

Figure 34.4 Black walnut branches tend to curve and grow irregularly.

In crystal vapour everywhere
Blue isles of heaven laughed between,
And far, in forest-deeps unseen,
The topmost elm-tree gather'd green
From draughts of balmy air.
    —Alfred, Lord Tennyson, "Sir Launcelot and Queen Guinevere"

35 SLIPPERY ELM

Red elm

Have you ever taken a slippery elm lozenge for a sore throat? That is just one of a large number of remedies and alternative medicine preparations that are derived from the inner bark of slippery elm, with folk remedies promising to cure everything from bladder infections to tapeworms.

WHERE TO LOOK FOR SLIPPERY ELM

Slippery elm is widely distributed and usually found where the soil is moist or rich, as on riverbanks or flood plains.

KEYS

- Reddish brown bark
- Slender branches
- Bitter scent

REDDISH BROWN BARK

References to slippery elm bark are usually to its inner bark, which is credited with many medicinal and healing properties. Should you find an injured tree, you could observe that the inner bark is a bright orange. Its outer bark is reddish brown to gray with rough sharp diagonal ridges that stand in high relief (Figure 35.1).

Figure 35.1 Slippery elm outer bark is reddish brown to gray with prominent sharp diagonal ridges. Note the roughness of their appearance.

SLENDER BRANCHES

If you are not sure about the bark, look up. If it is a slippery elm, its branches will be very long and very slender. Side branches are long and slender as well, giving the crown a very light and airy appearance (Figure 35.2).

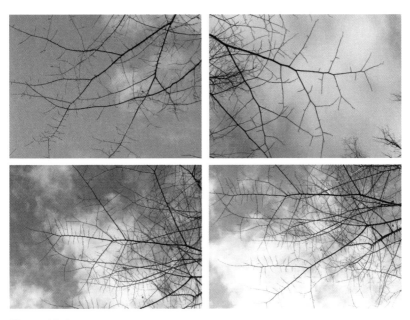

Figure 35.2 Slippery elm has long and slender branches.

BITTER SCENT

Like sweet and yellow birch, slippery elm is one of the trees that can be identified by scent when the bark is scratched off a twig, but where sweet and yellow birch have a pleasant wintergreen smell, slippery elm has a bitter smell.

As the spring comes on, and the densening outlines of the elm give daily a new design for a Grecian urn.

—Thomas Wentworth Higginson, *April Days*

36 AMERICAN ELM

Water elm, white elm

The American elm is often characterized as "stately." It is native to eastern North America. Although it graced many streets and yards in the past, Dutch elm disease, introduced to the United States in 1928, catastrophically decimated most of the trees. The disease was first recognized in the Netherlands, accounting for its name. It is caused by a fungus that is spread by the elm bark beetle. Nonetheless, American elms can still be found. There are some trees that have a natural resistance to the disease, and there are areas where the elm bark beetle has not appeared. A number of new Dutch elm disease–resistant cultivars have been developed; among them are Valley Forge, New Harmony, and American Liberty.

WHERE TO LOOK FOR AMERICAN ELM

American elms are hardy trees that can withstand temperature extremes from Canada to Florida. However, they are not found at higher elevations. Many are now found in urban settings: One of the largest and last stands of American elm is found in Central Park in New York City, and many are grown as landscape ornamentals.

- Classic vase shape

CLASSIC VASE SHAPE

American elms can be recognized by their classic vase-like shape (**Figure 36.1**). The trunk divides into limbs that grow upward close to one another and diverge slowly (there is no main trunk up high). Its branches hang down a bit at their ends.

Figure 36.1 American elm trees can be recognized by their stately vase-like profile. The lower right photograph shows a large American elm on the front lawn of the Vermont capitol.

Summer fervors slacken;
Sumac torches dim;
There's bronze upon the bracken;
September has a whim

—Katharine Lee Bates, "Playmates"

37 STAGHORN SUMAC

The red and hairy fruits (called "drupes") of the staghorn sumac provide feed for many animals and birds, and humans too. They can be
used to make a beverage called "sumac-ade" by soaking the drupes,
rubbing them, straining the juice, and sweetening it. (It is also called
"Rhus juice," as "Rhus" is sumac's scientific family name.) Sumac tea
can be brewed as well. You may have heard of poison sumac, but it is
quite different and can be identified by its white drupes. The velvety
branches of the staghorn sumac give it is name because of their resem-
blance to deer antlers.

WHERE TO LOOK FOR STAGHORN SUMAC

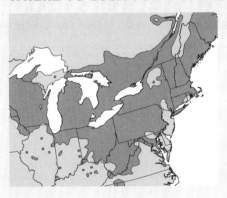

Staghorn sumac is found
throughout the Northeast with a
few exceptions. It does not tolerate shade and can typically be
found in burned areas, in open
fields, and along roadsides.

KEYS

- Red fruits (drupes)
- Velvet branches
- Form colonies

RED FRUITS (DRUPES)

The fruiting head of staghorn sumac starts in the spring as green but then turns red and persists through the winter (Figure 37.1).

Figure 37.1 The red fruiting heads of staghorn sumac are called drupes.

VELVET BRANCHES

The spikey nature of the branches and the velvet on them give the staghorn sumac its name because of their similarity to deer antlers (Figure 37.2).

Figure 37.2 Like deer antlers, staghorn sumac branches are velvety.

FORM COLONIES

Birds can feed on the fruits and seeds and then propagate the trees through their digestive tracts, but sumac also shoots up new trees from its roots (rhizomes), forming large stands or colonies of trees (Figure 37.3).

Figure 37.3 Staghorn sumac is often found in large homogenous colonies in which trees all share the same root system.

CONIFEROUS TREES

38 PINES

Although each pine has a number of distinguishing features as the following sections illustrate, the simplest way to recognize each one is by the number of needles in each bundle (Figure 38.1).

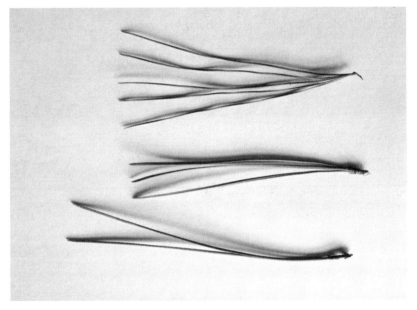

Figure 38.1 White pine, at the top, has five needles. Pitch pine, in the middle, has three needles. Red pine, at the bottom, has two needles that are longer than either red or pitch pine needles.

> Between every two pines is a door leading to a new world.
>
> —John Muir

39 WHITE PINE

Eastern white pine, northern white pine, soft pine

White pine is one of most useful and valuable trees in the forest. It helped build America as the virgin forests were logged and sawed into lumber. It grows fast and straight and is flexible, making it ideally suited for use as masts of sailing ships. In the old-growth forests of colonial days, white pine trees in the range of 200 feet tall, with trunks free of branches for 80 feet or more, were plentiful. The British, under King George I, claimed the tallest and largest white pines and marked them for the exclusive use of the British navy. Pine is also one of the more rapidly growing conifers, and is used in many reforestation projects.

WHERE TO LOOK FOR WHITE PINE

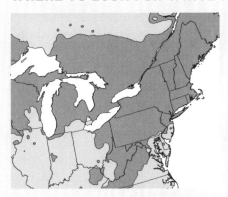

White pine appears throughout the Northeast, but only sparsely in Ohio, Indiana, and Illinois. It does not tolerate wet conditions. When young, it can be found growing in the open or at the edge of forests.

KEYS

- Five needles per bundle
- Pine bark
- Early adapter
- New leader each year

FIVE NEEDLES PER BUNDLE

White pine needles are bundled together, with five needles in each bundle (**Figure 39.1**).

Figure 39.1 White pine has five needles per bundle.

PINE BARK

Pine bark starts out smooth with a greenish cast and can be sticky with resin (**Figure 39.2**).

As the tree matures, the bark starts to get reddish brown and begins to furrow. Mature white pine bark is deeply furrowed with wide ridges. However, the ridges are broken horizontally into blocky rectangles (**Figure 39.3**).

RECOGNIZING TREES OF THE NORTHEAST

Figure 39.2 Young white pine bark starts off with a greenish cast, and sometimes resin seeps through the bark and appears white when dried.

Figure 39.3 Mature pines with deep furrows and wide ridges that are broken up horizontally into blocky rectangles.

EARLY ADAPTER

Trees that are the first species to seed into open areas are called "early adapters" or "pioneer species." White pine is one of them (**Figure 39.4**). As a forest grows up around it, it competes for sun by growing rapidly and straight up.

Figure 39.4 White pine is an early adapter, one of the first trees to appear in a clearing.

NEW LEADER EACH YEAR

White pines grow in a very regular pattern. At the top a single spike, called a "leader," grows straight up in one year. The next year, branches grow out sideways from the top of the leader, forming a layer, while a new leader grows straight up. The following year, the process repeats itself (**Figure 39.5**). The same is true of the branches. Thus, it is possible to determine the age of a pine tree by counting the number of leader sections, with each section representing one year of growth. When hiking with children, I like to point this out and then challenge them to find a pine tree that is the same age as they are.

Figure 39.5 White pine tree growth proceeds in a regular manner—a leader, a plane of branches, a leader, a plane of branches, and so on. The tree's age can be determined by counting the number of sections between each layer of branches. If the tree is too tall, you can continue counting out a branch (as shown in the photo on the lower right). In the photo at the top left, you can see how vigorously this pine is growing from the distance between the branch planes and from the length of this year's leader.

Norway pine is the state tree of Minnesota. It was called "Norway" for the homeland of the men who logged it.

—The Gymnosperm Database

40 RED PINE

Norway pine

The Latin species name of the red pine—*resinosa*—denotes the resin that flows so freely when the bark is penetrated, such as when woodpeckers drill their holes (**Figure 40.1**). Turpentine was originally made from pine resin.

Figure 40.1 Resin flows from holes made by woodpeckers in red pine trees.

WHERE TO LOOK FOR RED PINE

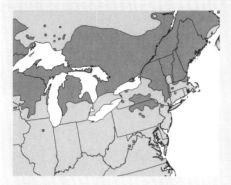

Red pine is reported throughout the Northeast but especially in the more northern areas and around the Great Lakes.

KEYS

- Bark has a red cast
- Two long needles in a bundle
- Needles and branch ends point upward
- Farmed red pine

BARK HAS A RED CAST

Red pine bark is similar to that of white pine, but side by side, their differences become apparent. One of the major differences is that red pine bark looks redder (**Figure 40.2**). As it matures, it becomes less red, but the red color can still be seen in the bark's furrows. Also, the scales of red pine trees can easily be picked off, whereas those of white pines cannot.

Figure 40.2 Red pine bark (left) gets its name from its varying degrees of red-
ness. It contrasts with the darker bark of white pine (right).

TWO LONG NEEDLES TO A BUNDLE

The needles of red pine are quite long—four to five inches. There are two needles in each bundle (Figure 40.3).

Figure 40.3 Red pine has two long needles per bundle.

NEEDLES AND BRANCH ENDS POINT UPWARD

Red pine needle bundles are clustered at the ends of twigs. These twigs tend to curve upward, which means that the needles point upward, too (Figure 40.4).

Figure 40.4 Red pine needles are clustered at the ends of twigs and, with the twigs, tend to point upward.

FARMED RED PINE

One can still find red pine planted on a grid in the Northeast (Figure 40.5). Red pine plantations were planted as reforestation projects and on pastureland that was no longer needed for grazing. In fact, in the 1920s, Robert Frost planted 1,000 red pines on his land in Vermont. Demand for telephone poles made red pine a cash crop. Today it is primarily planted for timber and pulpwood.

Figure 40.5 In New England, red pine plantations can still be found.

> The first and most natural way of lighting the houses of the
> American colonists, both in the North and South, was by the
> pine-knots of the fat pitch-pine, which, of course, were found
> everywhere in the greatest plenty in the forests.
>
> —Alice Morse Earle, *Home Life in Colonial Days*

41 PITCH PINE

Black pine

The "pitch" in "pitch pine" refers to its high resin content, which makes it rot-resistant. Because of the resin, knots of it have been used as torches, as referenced by Alice Morse Earle above. Stands of pitch pine are aptly called fire-dependent ecosystems. They depend on fire because their cones cannot release seeds until they are heated to a very high temperature. Even if all the needles burn off a tree in a fire, it will grow a new crown over the next several years.

WHERE TO LOOK FOR PITCH PINE

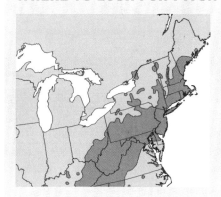

Pitch pine occupies a variety of habitats, from dry, acidic, sandy uplands to swampy lowlands. It can survive in very poor soil conditions, and because fire might kill other trees, pitch pine can survive and establish forests exclusively of pitch pine, such as those on Cape Cod (see **Figure 41.1**) or in the New Jersey Pine Barrens.

Figure 41.1 Pitch pine monocultures on Cape Cod.

KEYS

- Three needles
- Needles grow out from the trunk and branches

THREE NEEDLES

Pitch pine needles are much longer than white pine or red pine needles, and they come three-to-the-bunch (**Figure 41.2**).

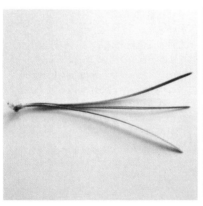

Figure 41.2 Pitch pine has three long needles per bunch.

NEEDLES GROW OUT FROM THE TRUNK AND BRANCHES

Although pitch pine can be identified by the fact that it has three needles per bundle, the easiest and most singular way to identify it is by the fact that its needles can grow directly out of its bark, whether on the trunk or branches (**Figure 41.3**).

Figure 41.3 Pitch pine needles can grow right out of the bark.

Hemlock-tree! O hemlock-tree! how faithful are thy branches!
Green not alone in summer time,
But in the winter's frost and rime!
O hemlock-tree! O hemlock-tree! how faithful are thy branches!
—Old German folk song, translated by Henry Wadsworth Longfellow

42 HEMLOCK

Eastern hemlock, Canada hemlock

The hemlock juice that Socrates drank is not from the hemlock tree. It was from a plant that has the same name because its smell is similar to that of crushed hemlock needles. Hemlock trees do not mature until they are 200 to 300 years old, and they can live to 800 years. Because its flat foliage catches and holds the snow, deer are likely to winter under hemlock. Hemlock trees were decimated in the Catskill Mountains of New York State and the Allegheny Mountains of Northern Pennsylvania in the 1900s, when their bark was stripped for its tannin, used in tanning leather. They are again being decimated today, this time by the hemlock woolly adelgid, an aphid that feeds on the tree.

WHERE TO LOOK FOR HEMLOCK

Hemlock is often found in mature, homogenous stands. Because it can tolerate shade, look for it on the northern slopes of mountains or in ravines.

KEYS

- Needles and branches lie flat
- Bark differences
- Droopy
- Climax forest

NEEDLES AND BRANCHES LIE FLAT

The flat single needles of the hemlock are attached on opposite sides of the twig. Their form is echoed by the structure of the branches, which are also formed in flat planes (Figure 42.1).

Figure 42.1 On hemlock, the needles are flat (left) and the branch form is flat as well (right).

BARK DIFFERENCES

With its scales, hemlock bark is fairly distinctive when it is young (Figure 42.2). However, when it matures, there is a lot of variation in how those scales coalesce into ridges. In some cases, it is difficult to distinguish mature hemlock bark from white pine bark, though with experience it is not so hard. Hemlock bark tends to be darker and browner than pine. Regardless of the bark, examining the needles and form is sufficient for identification.

Figure 42.2 The scaly bark of young hemlocks is shown in the top row. At the bottom are two variations of mature hemlock bark.

DROOPY

Hemlock branches are flexible and thus tend to droop downward. The same holds true for its leader at the top, which tends to flop over (**Figure 42.3**).

Figure 42.3 Hemlock branches are not rigid when young, so unlike spruce and fir, the ends of branches tend to droop or nod, as does the leader on top.

CLIMAX FOREST

Hemlock is the opposite of a pioneer species. Its seeds can germinate in the shade of an established forest. Hemlocks grow slowly, but as they mature, their dense foliage begins to shade the trees around them, eventually outliving those trees and leaving behind a homogenous forest of hemlock. Hemlock needles are highly acidic, and when they drop on the ground, they acidify the soil, which limits the growth of other trees and plants, thereby helping the hemlock to outcompete other species. Once a hemlock forest is established, almost nothing can grow under it but other hemlocks. By "climax forest" we mean that a hemlock forest is the last stage in the evolution of a forest; once the forest comprises only hemlock, it will remain unchanged until it is attacked by fire, storms (wind/ice), disease, logging, or, after many centuries, natural death (Figure 42.4).

Figure 42.4 Hemlock outcompetes almost all other trees, so almost nothing grows in the understory of a pure stand of hemlock.

I love to lie, when lulling breezes stir
The spiry cones that tremble on the fir.

—John Leyden, "Noontide"

43 BALSAM FIR

Eastern fir, Canadian fir, Christmas tree

Balsam fir is a boreal species, meaning that it occurs in the north, where it is able to survive the severe weather found there, and at higher elevations. It is primarily used as pulpwood. Like pitch pine, its resinous knots were used as torches. In the past, its sticky resin has been used both as a chewing gum and as a bandage for battle injuries.

WHERE TO LOOK FOR BALSAM FIR

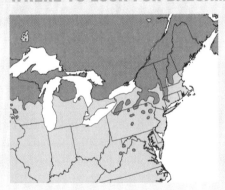

Balsam fir can be found in the northern reaches of the Northeast. It is found primarily at high elevations and in the boreal forest.

KEYS

- Familiar aroma
- Two white stripes on the back of its needles
- Bark is blistered, often with signs of resin on it
- Cones upright on branches
- Needles attached spirally

FAMILIAR AROMA

We recognize the fragrant aroma of fir trees from their use as Christmas trees and as a popular scent for such things as air fresheners and candles. Balsam fir's attractive form and dark green appearance make it one of the most popular trees for Christmas, with the added benefit that its needles stay on the tree for long periods. It takes eight to ten years to grow a six- to seven-foot Christmas tree.

TWO WHITE STRIPES ON THE BACK OF ITS NEEDLES

Perhaps the easiest way to identify Balsam fir is to look on the underside of the needles, where two white lines can be found (**Figure 43.1**).

Figure 43.1 There are two white lines on the undersides of balsam fir needles.

BARK IS BLISTERED, OFTEN WITH SIGNS OF RESIN ON IT

Balsam fir can also be identified solely by its bark. It is smooth but densely covered with blisters or bumps (**Figure 43.2**). The bark can ooze a sticky white resin that is sometimes used to mount specimens for viewing under a microscope.

RECOGNIZING TREES OF THE NORTHEAST

Figure 43.2 The bark of balsam fir showing blisters; it can sometimes ooze a sticky resin.

CONES UPRIGHT ON BRANCHES

Unlike the cones on most other conifers, balsam fir cones, when present, stick up from the branches rather than hang down.

NEEDLES ATTACHED SPIRALLY

The needles on a balsam fir lie flat, but when examined closely, it can be seen that the needles are actually attached around the twig in a spiral (**Figure 43.3**).

Figure 43.3 Although balsam fir needles lie flat, they are attached in a spiral around the twig.

I knew that when they stood up to hobble home, he would lead a few feet ahead, and she would follow. They grew up in the bush and still walked the same way, as if the wide road was nothing more than a narrow path through the muskeg and spruce.
—Joseph Boyden, *Through Black Spruce*

44 SPRUCE

I once was in a shop that specialized in the various species of wood used by musical instrument makers. Several men were holding sheets of spruce up to their ears and tapping them to judge the tone they made so they could select the best ones to use as guitar tops. Spruce wood is light and straight-grained. Like pine, it is also used for lumber. Apart from their different distributions (see maps below), the differences between red and white spruce are subtle enough that we can discuss them both simply as spruce.

WHERE TO LOOK FOR SPRUCE

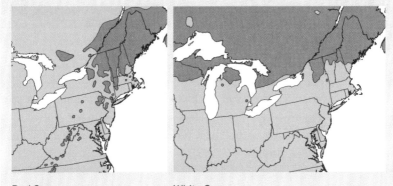

Red Spruce   White Spruce

Both red spruce and white spruce are most commonly found in northern latitudes as part of the boreal forest. Red spruce appears in the most northeasterly part of the region and at higher elevations down through the Appalachian Mountains. If a spruce is growing in a swamp, it is a black spruce—otherwise, it is a red or a white spruce.

KEYS

- Needles and form are spikey
- Bark comprised of small scales

NEEDLES AND FORM ARE SPIKEY

Spruce trees have fairly rigid branches and twigs. The leaders (top sections) point straight up. This gives the tree a spikey appearance (**Figure 44.1**).

Figure 44.1 Spikey spruce with erect leader and rigid branches.

The spikey form carries over to the needles. They are short and stiff and pointed (**Figure 44.2**). The tips feel sharp to the finger. Notice also that the needles encircle the twig, as opposed to balsam fir, whose needles lie flat in a plane.

Figure 44.2 Spruce needles are short, stiff, and pointed, and they encircle the twig.

BARK COMPRISED OF SMALL SCALES

Spruce bark may vary in color, but it is always comprised of small scales (Figure 44.3).

Figure 44.3 Spruce bark showing small scales.

45 HOW TO TELL SPRUCE FROM BALSAM FIR

KEYS

- Balsam fir bark has blisters, unlike spruce
- Spruce is spikey, fir is friendly
- Roll the needles between your fingers

BALSAM FIR BARK HAS BLISTERS, UNLIKE SPRUCE

One glance at the bark is enough to determine whether a tree is a fir or not because of the obvious blisters (Figure 45.1).

Figure 45.1 Balsam fir bark, on the left, has obvious blisters, unlike spruce, on the right.

SPRUCE IS SPIKEY, FIR IS FRIENDLY

There are two ways to tell spruce from fir using touch. If you touch the end of a needle, spruce will feel pointed and sharp. Fir, on the other hand, has rounded needle tips that are not sharp (**Figure 45.2**). A good way to remember this is, "Spruce is spikey, fir is friendly."

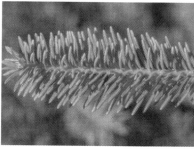

Figure 45.2 Spruce (left) has sharply pointed needles, while balsam fir needles (right) are soft and rounded at the ends.

ROLL THE NEEDLES BETWEEN YOUR FINGERS

Another way to tell whether a tree is a spruce or a fir by touch is to try to roll a needle between your fingers. Spruce needles are four-sided and can easily be rolled. Fir needles are flat, and you will not be able to roll them.

Thus yields the cedar to the axe's edge,
Whose arms gave shelter to the princely eagle.
—William Shakespeare, *Henry VI, Part III*

46 CEDAR

Arborvitae, northern white cedar, swamp cedar

There are several types of cedar commonly found in the Northeast: red cedar, white cedar, and Atlantic white cedar. All three of them are fairly similar, and if you can recognize one of them, you should be able to recognize all of them. Despite their similarities, however, each of the three belongs to a different family. Strangely, none of the native North American cedars belong to the cedar family (*Cedrus*), but the common name for all of them is "cedar." To learn to recognize cedar, we focus on the northern white cedar, which is also called "arborvitae," meaning "tree of life," presumably because it cured Jacques Cartier's explorers of scurvy. As a result, it was exported to Europe.

WHERE TO LOOK FOR CEDAR

White Cedar   Red Cedar

White cedar is widespread in the northern latitudes, although it appears sporadically in the more southern areas. It can grow in different soil types, including wetlands, giving it the common name "swamp cedar." Red cedar tends to populate the area south of where white cedar grows, and Atlantic white cedar, another species, is found sporadically along the coast from Maine to Delaware. Atlantic white cedar is prominent on Cape Cod and along the coast of New Jersey.

KEYS

- Vertical strips in the bark
- Flattened sprays of scaly leaves
- Tiny cones

VERTICAL STRIPS IN THE BARK

The bark of white cedar appears somewhat shreddy and fibrous, with vertical strips peeling away, and the pattern sometimes spiraling around the tree (**Figure 46.1**). The bark color can range from gray to red.

Figure 46.1 The bark of cedar trees appears as vertical strips that sometimes spiral around the trunk. It can range from gray to red.

FLATTENED SPRAYS OF SCALY LEAVES

The foliage of white cedar comprises flat sprays of tiny, scaly needles. The needles appear opposite each other, and the branches look like small trees (Figure 46.2).

Figure 46.2 The flat foliage of the northern white cedar.

TINY CONES

Cedar cones are very small and sit upright on the branch (Figure 46.3).

Figure 46.3 Upright cones of northern white cedar.

Give me of your roots, O Tamarack!
Of your fibrous roots, O Larch-Tree!
My canoe to bind together,
So to bind the ends together
That the water may not enter,
That the river may not wet me!
—Henry Wadsworth Longfellow, "The Song of Hiawatha"

47 TAMARACK

Larch, hackmatack

Native Americans had many uses for tamarack trees: From both the outer and inner bark, they made teas, flour, and poultices for a wide variety of medicinal and wound treatments. They boiled the roots to make them flexible and wove baskets from them, and they cleverly used bunches of tamarack twigs to make goose decoys. Its wood was traditionally used in boat building and, because of its strength and rot resistance, for exterior uses such as fence posts and decking.

WHERE TO LOOK FOR TAMARACK

Tamarack can be found as far north as central Alaska, as well as in the northern parts of the Northeast. The Ojibwa word for tamarack is *muckigwatig*, which means "swamp tree"—and indeed it is commonly found in swamps and bogs.

KEYS

- Short clusters of needles
- Loses its needles in the winter

SHORT CLUSTERS OF NEEDLES

Tamarack needles appear in small clusters or tufts and are quite short (Figure 47.1).

Figure 47.1 Tamarack needles form in small clusters.

LOSES ITS NEEDLES IN THE WINTER

Tamarack needles turn a glorious yellow to orange to brown in the fall and stay on the limbs until late fall or early winter. Then—and this may come as a surprise—this conifer, this tree with needles, a tree we might call "evergreen," loses all of its needles in the winter and appears to be dead (Figure 47.2). Nonetheless, come spring, the needles return.

Figure 47.2 Tamarack needles turn bright colors well into fall or early winter and then fall off, leaving the tree bare and looking dead.

STATE TREES

State trees are proposed to the legislature in each state, which makes the final selection. Two of the states covered by this book—Connecticut and Vermont—feature their state tree on their state quarter.

Connecticut: White oak
Indiana: Tulip poplar
Maine: White pine
Massachusetts: American elm
Michigan: White pine
New Hampshire: Paper birch
New Jersey: Northern red oak
New York: Sugar maple
Ohio: Ohio buckeye
Pennsylvania: Eastern hemlock
Rhode Island: Red maple
Vermont: Sugar maple
West Virginia: Sugar maple

CHAMPION TREES

Champion trees are those that are the biggest exemplars of their species. Lists of state champions are maintained in each state, and the organization American Forests keeps the list of national champions.

How big a tree is is carefully calculated by measuring the height of the tree, its diameter at breast height, and the spread of its crown. A standard formula is then used to combine these measurements and calculate the number of points for each tree, and the tree with the most points is designated the champion of that species.

The largest national champion is the General Sherman, a giant Sequoia in California's Sequoia National Park. It is 275 feet tall with a circumference of 103 feet near its base. The first branch is 130 feet above the ground. It is estimated that it weighs about 2.5 million pounds and is 2,000 years old. (From ring counts, it has been determined that other sequoias are more than 3,000 years old.)

Search for "champion trees" and your state name to find a list of the champions in your state.

The national champions of each species can be found at american forests.org.